CONFESSIONS *of the* ACCIDENTAL CAREER COACH

CONFESSIONS
of the
ACCIDENTAL
CAREER
COACH

**SURPRISING SECRETS *to* CREATE *a* LIFE-CHANGING JOB
HELPING OTHERS LAUNCH THEIR THRIVING CAREER**

Cara Heilmann

NEW YORK

LONDON • NASHVILLE • MELBOURNE • VANCOUVER

CONFESSIONS *of the* ACCIDENTAL CAREER COACH
SURPRISING SECRETS *to* CREATE *a* LIFE-CHANGING JOB
HELPING OTHERS LAUNCH THEIR THRIVING CAREER

© 2020 Cara Heilmann

Published in New York, New York, by Morgan James Publishing in partnership with Difference Press. Morgan James is a trademark of Morgan James, LLC. www.MorganJamesPublishing.com

ISBN 978-1-64279-591-2 paperback
ISBN 978-1-64279-592-9 eBook
Library of Congress Control Number: 2019939864

Cover Design by:
Rachel Lopez
www.r2cdesign.com

Morgan James is a proud partner of Habitat for Humanity Peninsula and Greater Williamsburg. Partners in building since 2006.

Get involved today! Visit
www.MorganJamesBuilds.com

To my husband, Edgar. Thank you for, well, everything.

To my boys, Eric and Andrew. If an opportunity feels scary and exciting at the same time, here's my advice: do it.

Table of Contents

Introduction		*ix*
Chapter 1	Why Won't This Nagging Feeling Go Away?	1
Chapter 2	How I Accidentally Became a Career Coach	11
Chapter 3	What Is a Career Coach Anyway?	21
Chapter 4	Two Layers of a Cake	29
Chapter 5	How to Get Calls From Recruiters	37
Chapter 6	How to Get Invited to an Onsite Interview	51
Chapter 7	How to Get an Offer	63
Chapter 8	How to Set-Up Your Business	83
Chapter 9	How Do I Sell When I Hate Sales?	97
Chapter 10	When Things Get Hard	109
Chapter 11	What's It Like on the Other Side	119
Acknowledgments		*123*
About the Author		*127*

Introduction

You've helped people for years. People have come to you asking for advice on their résumé or interviews. You may be from a recruiting, HR, or leadership role, and because of your expertise and who you are as a person, people have come to you asking for your advice. And now you've had this feeling that you're meant to do something totally different and dedicate your life's work to helping others. The area which you feel might be your calling is as a career coach.

Still, you aren't sure you know exactly how to start a business as a career coach. You don't feel that you could just call yourself one. And although you know a lot about helping people get jobs—because you've landed jobs easily in the past or have hired many people yourself—you aren't exactly sure you know everything you need to know about career coaching.

The piece that worries you the most is that you aren't all that great at selling yourself. You can sell a product that your company makes, but your services? You aren't sure you can market yourself and, egad, manage a sales conversation. In fact, the thought of selling makes you nervous and a bit a hesitant. You don't like it when someone tries to sell you something. So how can you sell your own career coaching business?

That leads you to another problem. You've built your career for many years and demand a certain pay. How will you make ends meet with a career coaching business? You wonder if this can this be a full-time thing or just a dream.

If you are pondering these things, I wrote this book so that you can know that you can create a thriving career coaching business. I know this because I've done it. I've built a business to where I am earning more than I've ever earned in my career. I want to help you catapult your career coaching business because, if you are called to be a career coach, you should grab that dream.

Not everyone is called to do something so completely others-focused. Not everyone has that deep yearning to dedicate their lives to helping others. If you are called to help others, you should do it. We need more of you, more people who want to make a significant difference in this world, in the lives of others. More people who gain tremendous internal satisfaction when they've helped someone. We need more people like you. I wrote this book so you can build a healthy career coaching business and avoid all the mistakes I've made trying to build this business. I've gone down the wrong path several times by trying different marketing schemes, from swipe files to selling small tiny services first. And not all of these schemes worked. It wasn't a true reflection of who I am and what I am attempting to accomplish. These felt more click-bait than authentic, more bait-and-switch than filled with love. So, if you are excited about building a business that is a true reflection of your heart's desire and are willing to go about it in a way that is real and honest, then read on. This book is for you!

CHAPTER 1

Why Won't This Nagging Feeling Go Away?

It'd been a couple of years in my new job and the newness was already gone. I wished the challenge of starting a new job could stay for more than just a couple of years. The excitement used to last at least three years, but the happy ramp-up time was already over. Maybe I needed to find a new job again for a new challenge. Who are the players, what are the issues, what can we do quickly to fix, make better? I love the overwhelming feeling of making a difference, of showing my value quickly. But after only two years, I'd hit all the targets and rebuilt the processes. I'd hired all the staff and trained them to perform. Things were humming well. You'd think I'd be thrilled, but I was bored.

"You have that look on your face," said Kathy, my training manager.

"What look?" I asked.

"The look of wanting to stir things up," she playfully whispered, looking around in a conspiratorial way.

I heard what she was thinking, because I could read it on her face: "Why can't you just let things be?" It's such a great question, because it would be so easy to come in every day, do my thing, and then go home at night and forget about work. How great it would be to just flip on the maintenance switch and coast? I could see the question in Kathy's eyes: "Could we not have a new effort, please?" Yet there I was, meeting with my team to ask about complaints, murmurings, ideas of what we can do now. What campaign can we launch? What problem can we fix? What big hairy audacious giant can we slay?

Undeterred by the status quo, my team and I found a new activity to do. "It will re-energize the office!" I exclaimed to my boss, the Executive Director and CEO. It was dark in his corner office because I posted flipcharts up on every wall. I marched him through a justification of what we should do next. "What if we were to figure out what our core values are?" I asked. With a nod, he approved the campaign.

Excited that I had a new project to play with, I jumped in with both feet.

Six months later, everyone was proud of what we'd accomplished. But once again, I was bored and thinking of what could be done next. "This is a huge company. There must to be something else I could do," I said, believing I just needed a new problem to solve.

I joined national committees and immersed myself in the world of diversity and inclusion. I raised my hand to help with a national physician education program. I inserted myself where I wasn't wanted to keep the learning and excitement going. I orchestrated a LinkedIn training class for our physician recruiters. Another year went by, and I got bored again.

You might not be in the same vertical of human resources and recruiting, but does this sound like you? It is like an itch that never goes away. Like you are just lightly touching the edge of your life's work and never fully immersed. There are moments of alignment where the time flies by, but most of it feels like you are back in school watching the second-hand slowly move around the clock. Then, the boredom morphs into something else more negative.

It starts out just as a small feeling that something isn't right, like the spark and enjoyment of what you're doing just isn't there anymore. Going to work gets harder and harder.

Shawna—my assistant—and I have an inside joke. "Is it a fake it 'till you make it day?" we'd ask each other as we walked into the office. We'd trade a knowing look across the office. I love Shawna. She is brilliant and professional, and I know that this job is a stepping stone to something else for her. This is a stepping stone for something for me, too. Maybe that is why we get along so well; we are in the same boat. We both wondered what our next lily pad could be.

I thought working for a nonprofit in the healthcare industry would be the fuel that would keep my flame eternally bright. Making a difference in the lives of people through access and getting well is a great mission. It is. Yet, it felt like there was a knot in the pit of my stomach that kept me thinking I should be doing something more, something more meaningful.

I never got to the point where I said that I hated my job. I've talked with many people who have said that they hate their jobs. I was close. For me, it was more of a sense of dread and a lot of regret. Did I make the right choice in moving my entire family to Northern California for this job? Maybe I should've stayed where I was because we were growing a team, creating a department out of nothing. And it was also in the healthcare space. So many doubts filled my mind.

Sunday evenings were the worst. Right around four o'clock in the afternoon it would hit me that very soon I would need to go into the office again. It was when the sun started to sink below the horizon that the sinking feeling in the pit of my stomach would start. I knew that early tomorrow morning I would see Shawna, and she'd ask if it was one of those fake-it-make-it days. I'd do this, all the while dreaming that there must be something else that makes me happy.

"Have you thought about talking to a career coach?" asked Susanne, a colleague and friend.

We'd become close friends since attending an executive leadership intensive at the Harvard Business School. In Boston, we bonded. Susanne and I were on the same team of eight named high-potential healthcare executive minds. We spent evenings preparing and became close friends. Susanne is safe. She's someone I trust, so I know I could share my unhappiness with my job.

She said, "I may know someone who might be able to help sort it out; you should talk with her."

I didn't ask how she knew Mary, who is a career coach. I guessed that perhaps Susanne had talked with her too, long ago. I never asked Susanne, instead leaving that question unanswered. But it did make me feel better that someone so accomplished like Susanne had a career coach.

Mary was a breath of fresh air. From the first conversation, I liked Mary. She believed in me and that I am all I need to be, not needing to be anything more. We chatted every other week and I couldn't wait for our conversations. I shared that I was meant to do something else.

"Create your own job, Cara," said Mary. "Create a role filled with only the things that make you happy, that bring you joy."

Later I took out a blank sheet of paper and I started to write.

I loved it when I helped others one-on-one. I like teams, but really love it when I connect deeply with another person. Victoria, director of quality, was struggling in her role and her boss asked me to chat with her. She was exceptional at getting things done; however, she would unknowingly knock people aside while marching to the goal. I met Victoria for several weeks and loved it when it dawned on her that she was a bull and we were the china in the shop. I especially loved it when her boss praised her after Victoria made a few small changes to her approach. Victoria's boss said that she sent Victoria to "Cara's Charm School." It wasn't charm school. It was quite simple, really. All that happened is that Victoria realized that the person she is wasn't really coming through. The brilliant, talented, confident Victoria never made it past her skin. And what we were seeing was something else she thought we wanted to see. Once she understood this, she made a few tiny modifications and now we got to see the real Victoria.

I also loved it when I helped people get jobs. Searching for candidates is something I really loved to do. I loved to dig into online databases to find that one person that might be a great fit for the vacancy. And I especially loved it when I found a rare talent and made a connection with the hiring manager. Julie was the name of a possible candidate that I heard a couple of times and I wanted to talk with her. With her mobile number in hand, I call her and mentioned this role I have for an S.V.P. of H.R. She was intrigued. Two weeks later she met with our C.E.O. and they fell in love with each other (in a business way). It is a type of business match-making that I love.

I'm also critical of résumés. I've reviewed a hundred résumés of my friends, co-workers, and neighbors. I'd give my advice and often spend hours revising the résumé for them. I never charged a dime; instead, the currency came from the results. People would say things like, "Cara, thank you for helping my son with his résumé...he started work Monday as a Case Assistant." It made me feel great to know that I helped someone get a job. And, like Victoria, I loved knowing that I helped someone thrive in a job.

Per Mary's advice, I reviewed all that I love and everything that I wanted my new job to be.

"I want to do these things every day of my life," I told Mary.

Immediately, Mary said, "You should become a coach, like me."

Suddenly, I felt like the door of the cage was opened. The idea was so light and free. And yet it was like standing on the edge of a high cliff and with a long way down. This scary-exciting feeling filled my stomach, replacing the sour clenching feeling. Could I do it? Could I start my own business? Could I support myself as a career coach? I was not sure what to do. Where would I start? What would I need?

I had so many doubts. What would I call my business? Would someone buy from me? Do I need a website? Would I be credible? Would I make any money? I had so many doubts about my own abilities, even though I've started businesses in the past. The first business was in high school where I made figurines that I put on boxes and wrote the client's name in pretty lettering. That was loads of fun. I held parties at my house and my friends would come over and buy items for the holidays. I did this until my mom, who had a very successful thriving manufacturing business, asked me how much money I made.

"I made a ton of money," I said.

She raised her eyebrows and said, "Sit down, let's look at this."

When I added it all up, I didn't make any money at all. In fact, I now had a lot of inventory and was in the red, per my calculations. Remembering this first venture, all the doubts flooded in. How could I think I would make money now because I couldn't make money as a teenager? It's interesting how fear reminded me of my earliest failure as an entrepreneur.

Is it even possible to be like my mom, a successful businesswoman? I had more questions and doubts swirling in my mind. I spewed them all to Mary, explaining why it would just be a silly endeavor to strike out on my own because I had failed in the past. If only I could win the lottery, I'd be set. I could launch my career coaching business and not have to worry about profits.

As you know, I did make it. I do have a thriving coaching business; so much so that I have a list of prospects who want to talk with me on a waiting list that is four weeks long.

There's been a major shift in the way we see coaches, which has helped seasoned professionals turn to career coaches. Having a coach isn't something you have to hide. Before, I was hiding the fact that I had a career coach! I never mentioned Mary's name. Susanne and I never disclosed that she worked with a career coach as well. It was like some weird taboo subject that I needed to talk with a coach. Times are different! Millennials have grown up with coaches their entire lives—sports coaches, speech coaches, tutors to name a few—a coach is another extension of their learning community, their circle of support.

If you think about it, we have personal trainers who coach us to improve our athletic (and mental) skills. We have music teachers who help us learn an instrument. We have language instructors. We have people who surround us every day. Why not work with someone who can help your career? Today, it has become a smart thing to do to have a career coach. In fact, many companies are hiring career coaches to help their own employees find other jobs within the company, and without! People are clamoring for a great career coach, so much so that there is a line out the door to have a one-hour conversation with me.

We need more career coaches. We need more good career coaches in this world to help people find their path, stay on track, and feel like a million bucks every day.

This is my story. I didn't set out thinking I'd become a career coach. It is such a new field, and, in fact, today's career coaches are forming the profession. One of my colleagues created and is leading an international association of career coaches, the first of its kind. We are on the cutting edge, and if you feel like you are falling into this role, too, that you never thought you'd grow up to be a career coach, I get you! Like you, I just so happened to fall into this field, and it has changed my life. I love each day, I love the people I support and work with. I love the people I train. And when people ask what day it is, I don't know. To me, every day is Friday. And it can be Friday for you, too.

CHAPTER 2

How I Accidentally Became a Career Coach

This is Margaret's story. Margaret is a rock star. Every meeting I had with Margaret, she was prepared, engaged, and supportive. I considered Margaret to be my right-hand. Every human resource executive has two key resources that are essential to success. Margaret was one of those for me. Much of what we do in human resources is like what a marketing or communications department would for clients, or in our case, employees. If we see our employees as customers, a human resources executive shifts the talent that they need to be effective. Human resources and talent management requires a lot of communication to our employees and, in many companies, this role is called internal communication. Margaret was that for me. She was a Senior Communications Consultant within our organization, and I relied on her to help me get the message out. And not just telling but sharing the message in a way that our employees would digest in the way we intended. There are times when I'd send something out only for it to backfire. It didn't come across just the way I had wanted, and employees were now confused. This is where Margaret came in.

She was creative, pushed the boundaries on what we could do to get the message across. After reading or hearing what I wanted to communicate, Margaret helped me see the message through the eyes of the employees. She would often challenge the message. And challenge the venue or the channel through which I wanted to send the message. Remember the core values campaign that I pitched to my boss? Margaret had a very out of the box idea, or at least I thought it was unusual, to memorialize our values as a division.

"We should create a jacket for every single one of our employees," said Margaret. "It would add a level of identity to our division." Yes, and an expense to a budget that didn't want to support the burden. "A jacket?" I wondered. In the end, we handed out beautiful jackets with our brand and identity embroidered across the arms. Our employees loved them. They wore them everywhere. Like a letterman jacket, it carried a sense of pride.

I looked forward to my weekly meetings with Margaret, because even though she challenged the way I was wording something or even pushed-back on large strategic concepts, I always knew she was doing so with our employees' best interests in mind. Then, our meetings started to change.

Margaret was growing increasingly concerned about her job. Despite her success, and in my eyes, her talent, the company hired a manager above her. Now she was one layer removed from the V.P. of Communications. She began to worry about how the company saw her and worry that her new boss didn't appreciate her style of challenging ideas.

"I am not sure, Cara, I feel like maybe I am being pushed out of the company," she said. Worry was stamped across her eyes, and I could see that the strain of the thought weighed on her. Our weekly communication meetings turned into coaching sessions.

Together, we would think of different ways to help her manage her achievements to her new boss and try different things to work well with her new boss. When that would not work, we could create ways to gain her visibility with her V.P. of Communications, who used to be a strong advocate, but it seemed like that relationship had cooled. She doubled her efforts and doubled her work time so that everything was executed well. Everything was created with perfection in mind. Margaret wanted seamless execution. She went far beyond her job description to show her value to her new boss and the organization, so that positive comments would come back to her boss. Each time there was a bump in the road, Margaret would grow increasingly worried. Each week, I saw a different Margaret. She aged. The confidence she once had seemed to have left, and she now a look in her eyes of a deer in the forest, always darting back and forth.

That was when I did something I've never done before. I helped my rock star team player find another job outside of the company.

"Have you thought of applying elsewhere?" I asked her at our next meeting.

Her entire body stilled for a moment. Deciding what to tell the head of human resources. Wondering if she is in safe territory. What my reaction would be if she told the truth. She said quietly, as if the walls could hear her response, "Yes, I am looking." She had contacted the agency who placed her with us and was quietly getting the word out that she may be interested in other opportunities.

Our meetings took on a different tenor. No longer planning our next employee communication strategy, we went into Find Margaret a Job mode.

You might be thinking, "Of course Cara should help her find a new job!" However, I'd been trained in human resources to *keep* talent. Retention is key, especially for companies that take a long time to onboard new employees. In our world, it took someone nine months before they kind of got it at our company. Each new employee received a major investment in time to get them to just kind of getting it in their first year with us. To help someone leave, especially someone I considered to be a rock star, went against the grain.

I didn't understand what was going on with Margaret's manager or why Margaret's new boss didn't get it. They didn't see what a rock star she is. Margaret and her boss were cut from different fabrics. He was cut from the same fabric of the organization: looks right, sounds right, goes with the flow. Margaret was nothing like that. She was her own person and came with ideas that were years ahead of anyone's vision in the room. I came to realize that although I needed her, and that she was a rock star in my eyes, this company wasn't the best place for her. In fact, if she were to stay, she'd shrink over time. Our culture didn't allow her to be her. It required a sense of conforming, a mold for the employee to fit within a certain shape and size. I saw this clearly with Margaret.

It was then that I came to believe that there is a place where everyone belongs, that in one company, someone could be a rock star and then that same person could go to another company and be mediocre. Just average. Or worse, that the culture of the organization does more to spur productivity than nurture the talent that we recruit.

It was then that I realized that these unseen forces, the culture as we call it today, created a cage. And Margaret was trying to live in that cage. And that I was also trying to be in my own cage.

I realized that all I wanted to accomplish, the big ideas that I had were never going to come to fruition because I also had to conform—to look the part, sound the part, to be the part. I understood in that moment why, when I bumped into colleagues outside of work, I didn't recognize them. They looked like different people. "Stephanie? Is that you?" Seeing her out of context threw me; however, her face beamed as she said, "Hi! Yes! I'm a different person outside of work. This is the real me." That a culture can shape productivity can also stop us from being authentic.

It was at that moment that I started to meet with Mary, my coach. When I could see that if I were to stay, I would have to start bending like origami and trying to fit myself into a culture that would require me to be someone else, someone unlike who I am. It was time to change something. I met with one of the co-founders of the Covey Institute, and as we were going over my leadership style profile, he said, "You need to be careful, Cara, because per your profile, you'll never be understood in a traditional corporate environment."

It was time for me to leave.

I grouped all that I loved in my twenty-plus years and created a job, a role that I want meant to fulfill. It was at that point that I became a career coach.

I wish I could say that I never looked back, but I did. Two times after I hung my shingle, I looked back.

Once when I got an InMail out of the blue from someone who liked my LinkedIn profile. She was looking for a Chief Talent Officer for her start-up. I took down my coaching shingle and accepted a contract job. It didn't even last a year, because as soon as I started, I felt that feeling of dread again that I was back in a cage.

So, when a friend of mine reached out to me looking for a V.P. of Operations for her Hawaii office, I further buried my shingle and accepted the job. That didn't last a year as well. I continued to feel that there is more for me. Things that were bigger, more meaningful to me. I yearned for my coaching clients. I missed my job seekers. And when I turned in my resignation, it was for the last time. I reached into my closet, dusted off my shingle, and hung it once again. And it hasn't come down since.

Business took off. I wrote my first book, *The Art of Finding the Job You Love: An Unconventional Guide to Work with Meaning*. I hired a marketing talent. I hired a business coach. And since then have helped hundreds of people as a career coach. At the time of writing this book, I have helped well over 800 people with their careers. I helped a hotel on the island of Maui that shut its doors help their employees prepare for new jobs. On one day, 400 employees at this amazing four-star resort emptied their employee lockers for the last time. I helped this company end this chapter and care for its employees with love. I'm currently helping a large healthcare firm create an internal career coaching division to help with redeploying talent within their company in light of a layoff. Don't send them out into the world; let us find them new homes within our organization. And I'm training the next generation of independent career coaches. Teaching them all that I know so that more and more people can have the opportunity of working with a qualified professional career coach.

I call this training process The Career Coach Accelerator, teaching people exactly what I am doing so they can start thriving coaching businesses from the first day they hang their shingle. My goal is to help them avoid all the mistakes I made when I first set up and started running a coaching business.

There are two skills that are needed to have a thriving coaching business. The first is the technical know-how of being a career coach, the ability to help people answer the question, "What should I do when I grow up?" The skill to look at an online profile and know exactly how to optimize it so that recruiters find the person.

The second is the knowledge of running a business. What to name the business. What form to first start the business. How to sell when you aren't a sales person. These two skills are what I will share with you in this book: technical skill and business skill.

I will share with you all the technical skills you will need to support your clients. And I will share all the business operations skills you will need to run a profitable thriving career coaching business so that you can help people like Margaret find the right company fit.

By the way, Margaret landed a role shortly after we talked about her finding another role. She said it felt like years before she landed in her new job, but it was only a couple of months. She accepted a job as a Senior Manager of Internal Communications at an international financial services company. That was seven years ago. Today, she is the Global Director of Internal Communications at this firm. She reports directly to the C.E.O. and has a very strong working relationship with the V.P. of Human Resources. She has transformed the financial services firm from one with low employee engagement scores to holding multiple international awards for employee engagement. Best Place to Work for multiple years. Glassdoor Best C.E.O. list. Last I counted, this company had twelve different awards, all earned after Margaret started at the company. I know her C.E.O. knows that she was the number one person responsible for these awards. She brought out the C.E.O.s voice and tailored messages to millennials, the bulk of their employees, and challenged legacy ideas of communicating with the employees. She moved communication from email to mobile and eliminated archaic policies prohibiting employees from going on social media during work and using work equipment. She created a socially connected organization and pushed communications across the ways in which employees get their information today. YouTube.

Twitter. Instagram. She did all this, while also building a high-performing internal communications team.

Margaret convinced me that there is a place for everyone. Everyone has talents and, in the right culture, the right company, can be the superstar that they are.

Career coaches can help them navigate that path to find what they are meant to do in this world and the culture in which they would thrive. To put that job in what I call a Career G.P.S. and identify the paths to reach that end destination. To see that one path will take a long time while another path is fraught with many speed bumps, but that there is this one path that is a straight shot even knowing that it may take one or two jobs to get there, but now the person has a plan: a career plan. And the career coach can be right alongside that person helping them identify and achieve that plan.

But, before I dive into exactly how to do that, it is important to define what a career coach is. There are many coaches on the scene, from life coaches to relationship coaches to spiritual coaches. What is the difference between each of these modalities? And which one is best for you?

CHAPTER 3

What Is a Career Coach Anyway?

There are many different types of coaches today. By the time that this book is in print, I bet there will be many more. Close to the realm of career coaches, there are life coaches, business coaches, executive coaches, spiritual coaches, and relationship coaches. Here are a few of my definitions of each type of coach.

Life coaches work with their clients to help them in all areas of their lives, helping them overcome obstacles and make personal shifts to find resonance in all areas. A life coach may touch upon career from the strategic view of the person's overall direction and well-being.

Business coaches work with clients to help them grow their business. Business coaches help clients take their business from where it is now to where the owner would like it to be. It dives into creating a vision, goals, and objectives for the business. It can touch all aspects of being a business owner, from leadership to marketing to finance to sales.

Executive coaches work with clients to enhance and develop leadership and management performance. The executive coach may focus on the skills the executive needs to build and lead a team to achieve the executive's goals. It may touch upon talent and skill fit for a role with the intent to develop the skills to perform at a higher leadership level.

Spiritual coaches work with clients to identify a spiritual direction and deepen their spiritual connection. Spiritual coaches go deeper than behaviors and touch upon deeply rooted beliefs and connections to God and/or the divine. They may touch upon careers insofar as its alignment with the client's spiritual direction.

Relationship coaches work with clients to build healthy, thriving relationships. They help people define their relationship goals and support them in achieving the goals. Relationship coaches could work with two or more people, or individuals wanting coaching for relationships.

Finally, career coaches work with clients to identify career direction and the skills needed to get that job and build a career. Career coaches have skills to revise a résumé, to network, to prepare for interviews, to prepare them to have a great start in the new role and to grow in their role. My favorite nonprofit, Wardrobe for Opportunity, has a tag line that sums it up: "get a job, keep a job, and build a career."

Through the definitions, you can see the differences and overlaps. Life coaches have the broadest definition, as it touches all areas of a person's life. It is the "generalist" of all coaches, as it could touch upon spirituality, relationships, career, and so forth. With that comes the challenge of monetizing a life coaching business. What is the R.O.I. to a person for the amount paid for life coaching? It is easier to see an R.O.I. for business coaching and career coaching. Harder for life coaching because what is the goal? Is there a binary end point where you know you've received a R.O.I.?

The reason why I started to train career coaches is that three close colleagues, all certified life coaches, came to me asking to teach them the skills of career coaching. These three brilliant individuals—Mary, Edith, and Curt—became my advisory team as I built the curriculum for The Career Coach Accelerator. Almost every client had an aspect of career that was discussed, and yet, a sense that they weren't sure they knew how to revise a LinkedIn profile, for example.

I was trained as a life coach. I studied with the Coaches Training Institute in San Rafael and loved every minute of it.

However, I didn't get my certification as a life coach because I knew I wanted to focus on the slice of career. I ended up getting a certification as a career coach and eventually created my own curriculum for a senior level career coach—finding the current career coaching certification programs great for people with little work experience or understanding of how people get jobs. I find that once someone has about seven years of work experience, they are ready for a senior level certification training program.

One thing that is similar between all the coaches is that we are not therapists who work with clients to help them find resolution to past problems and help them move forward. Therapists, or sometimes called counselors, are healthcare professionals who work on a long-term basis to diagnose and resolve past issues. Therapists focus on the past. Coaches focus on the present and tend to be more short-term relationships. Coaches are not healthcare professionals. We start from today, create clear objectives, and run alongside the client to achieve those objectives.

Of all the skills that are taught as a career coach, the item that brings the most angst is the résumé. I hear this question from future career coaches: "Do I have to revise résumés?" They hate to revise their own résumé, and this trauma makes them wonder if they have the skills to write and revise other people's résumés. All I can say is that it is much easier writing someone else's résumé. It is hard to write about ourselves. Don't fret, I'll share with you my tips and hacks to writing résumés as quickly as possible! The question about résumés always leads to a question: "What is the best background to have to be a great career coach?"

Intuitively one would think that a background in human resources or recruiting might be the best. Although understanding different roles within an organization (which someone in human resources would) might be an advantage, I've found that many people have a different perspective. Someone in a central function, like finance, would also have this wide purview. And I have found that when someone is in a leadership role, they also have this wide perspective.

However, even individuals within one job in one silo end up being some of the best career coaches. For example, Michelle is a procurement specialist and has been at her current company for fifteen years. She's never done anything but procurement at her company, so she doesn't even have another company's structure or process to have as a background. Her niche is helping individuals who want to leave the military translate their experience on their documents and the interview in a way that someone outside the military would understand. She grew up in a family of individuals from many different branches of the military. Her husband was in both the Army and Marines. She is intimately familiar with all of the acronyms and military jargon that would cause someone else to scratch their head. She is a perfect career coach for her niche, and because of that, it makes her an outstanding career coach to help individuals transitioning out of the military.

She may not know all of the roles out there; however, Michelle is smart and found a community of like-minded career coaches, and she leverages their experience to help her and her clients.

It is true that recruiters find this work familiar. It is the reverse or the other side of the table of what they are doing today. However, it is exactly this perspective that makes it a bit harder for them. Recruiters see the world looking for round pegs that fit round holes. They quickly assess a person's background to see if the person is a fit for their vacancy. It takes a bit to turn the tables, to turn the perspective to look at this from the perspective of a job seeker.

Bottomline, I find that if you have about seven years of work experience, you have enough work experience to be a great career coach. And if you find a niche that really touches your heart, like Michelle did with individuals in the military, you could really become invaluable to your clients.

If you are still reading, chances are you are still interested in becoming a career coach. You are trying to figure out what might be your niche and the strengths you'll bring to your clients. We will cover all of those areas in the chapter after next. What we will cover in the next chapter is a dive into the pool of building skills as a career coach, from helping someone answer the question, "What should I do when I grow up?" to helping them network to preparing for interviews in a way that will land them the job.

And whether to start your own career coaching business or to just improve existing skills to help your family members and friends, I hope that you will find the next chapters to be educational as well as inspirational.

CHAPTER 4

Two Layers of a Cake

There are two layers of skill required to have a thriving career coaching business: helping clients get jobs and establishing your own business. This is where I see many career coaches fail. They either don't have one layer or the other. They think that they only need one layer, usually the first layer of skill, and do not pay enough attention to the second layer of what it takes to establish a business. This chapter will outline the two layers and set the stage for the subsequent chapters that will go into further detail.

THE FIRST LAYER

The first layer represents the fundamental skills to help a client get a job. It is what clients are seeking when they reach out asking for help. How do I identify my career path? What about my résumé should be changed? Can you help me come across with confidence? What about preparing for interviews? The best way for us to tackle the skills is to look at the overall process of landing a job. It is this layer that many people feel like they have the skills.

For example, Jason is an executive recruiter at a healthcare company. He started The Career Coach Accelerator a bit skeptical, because he thought he had all the skills needed to be a career coach. In fact, he said, "I bet I could hang my shingle today and start taking clients." After three days into The Career Coach Accelerator, Jason was asking the most questions. He was the most interested in the next area, realizing that there is a lot more to becoming a career coach than a lifetime as a recruiter.

Let's stand on the top of the trees. From a strategic view, there are three hurdles a job seeker must clear before getting a job:

- Getting a call from a recruiter
- Getting invited to an interview
- Getting an offer

Like a track-and-field race, one misstep would be a fault and possible ejection from the rest of the race. In order to progress, the job seeker must successfully clear the first hurdle, then the next, and then the last. Rarely do people go straight from the first to the last hurdle. It is a typical job search process and because of this, it is easier for us to help our clients build the necessary skills to progress from one hurdle to the next.

GETTING A CALL FROM A RECRUITER

The first step is to get that call. It could be an email or an InMail through LinkedIn, the largest online professional networking platform. This is the first step of the job search funnel (similar to a sales funnel because the job seeker is selling themselves, if you think about it). And it takes a great résumé, a great cover letter, a great online profile plus a ton of networking to get a call from a recruiter. Often job seekers can get a call without any of these documents, which I call the dossier (résumé, cover letter, online profile) by having a very solid connection with someone who networks for them into an organization. However, at some point in the process, the dossier will be requested by the recruiter. Of the three, the résumé is the most important piece of the entire dossier. We will review all the steps required to create a compelling dossier.

GETTING INVITED TO AN INTERVIEW

When I talk about an interview, I mean specifically an onsite interview. This is beyond the telephone screen or even the video conference screens that are more common today. This is standing or sitting in front of the people who make the decision whether to make you an offer or not. The onsite is usually with at least three people: always the hiring manager, sometimes a peer, and someone in human resources. The peer is there for a technical perspective. The human resources person for a "people" perspective. It might be the same person who conducted the screen, or another voice in the talent organization. Think about all the things that need to happen to get that invitation to interview. We will review the steps and skills that your client will need to learn to get an invitation to interview.

GETTING AN OFFER

This is the last step. This is after the onsite interview is completed and is the elusive chalice, the tape of the finish line, the prize to get. It is the goal of every single client. This means that your client nailed the interview. It sounds so simple, yet it is very difficult. It is unrealistic to think that the hiring manager knows all they need to know about a person from this one snapshot in time. It is like a performance, going on stage in front of an audience. It is one snapshot in time and because of this, sometimes one hour with each person, so many things can influence the performance. For example, your client had an off day or is fighting the flu or just had something tragic happen in their lives. They could've had a bad night of sleep the night before, or accidentally twisted their foot on the way in and the pain is a constant presence throughout the interview. And that is just on the job seeker side. So many things can happen on the other side as well, the hiring manager just got bad news, or someone got sick and so they had to ask someone else to sit in the interview process. We'll cover all that you can do to help your client best prepare for the interview so that they can put their best foot forward and show all that they can do and all they can contribute to the organization so that they can't see another day without that person as part of their team.

It seems so simple, yet each step requires a different skill and we will go through each one in the next chapter. Once you know the skills needed to help your client, which is the first layer, we'll cover the second layer, and that is what it takes to start and run a thriving coaching business. You could have the necessary skills and your coaching business could fail because you do not have the skills to run a thriving business.

THE SECOND LAYER

The second layer has three essential steps of establishing your business.

The first essential step would be the pre-work and decisions that need to be made before you hang your shingle. This starts with your niche and ends with the form of your company. I want to be clear from the get-go that all of my thoughts, all of my advice is coming from my own experience.

I'll share the mistakes and wasted time and money I threw away in establishing my own career coaching business. The goal is to help you get started as quickly as possible and starting to generate revenue quickly with the least amount of cost. You could hire a massive marketing firm to help you create a website and invest thousands of dollars doing so; however, that isn't want you are going to learn in this book. I am all about guerilla entrepreneurism. One with Lean start-up and Minimal Viable Product concepts infused so that you establish a business as quickly as possible with the least amount of start-up costs.

The second essential step is your offered program as a career coach. What are the processes you should establish? How long is your engagement with your client? How should you price your services? These decisions are all things that will change multiple times while you are open for business. You can have an idea going in; however, based on your niche, your life cycle stage (just started to establish), and your own style, you are going to make small and radical changes to your processes. This step is all about what are those steps that you should be considering and what might be the best way in which you deliver your service to your clients. This is where your creativity will really come alive. I've heard so many great ideas about how career coaches deliver their product, and I'll review of a few of them with you to help inspire you as you design your offering.

The third essential step is the piece which almost every single one of my career coaches are the most concerned about. How do I get business? I am going to cover my process of how I find and sell my coaching services. I think you'll be surprised at how tactic-free my sales process is. I don't have tricks or manipulative processes to lure people to sign on with me. It is based on a simple belief that people buy from people they like, and so if we come across as authentic and filled with love (yes, I just said love in a business book) then the sales will be higher. I'll cover with you my advertising, marketing, and sales processes so that you can close as many sales as you want to bring in the monthly revenue that translates to the annual income you are targeting. We all start with the end in mind, the annual amount we wish to hit because from there, we work backwards. More on this later. All I want to say now is that *sell* doesn't have to be a four-letter word. I look forward to every single one of my sales conversations and now you can too.

Let us start with the first conversion point, how to help you client get a call from a recruiter. It is where most of your clients are stuck. It is where most of your clients will finally say, "I need help and I can't do this alone." The world has changed. The way in which we find jobs is completely different today than it was fifteen years ago. Heck, even ten years ago! There are tech advances like machine learning and artificial intelligence that are changing the landscape of finding a job, and the next chapter will teach you how you can help your client get that call they are seeking from a recruiter.

CHAPTER 5

How to Get Calls From Recruiters

By the time I met Mark, he was out of work for nine months without a single interview. Nothing was wrong with his background—with a master's degree and a juris doctorate, he was an attorney by trade. My first conversation with Mark, I found him to be a great communicator which supported his background of being a litigation attorney. But why in the world, after nine months and sending hundreds of applications (he actually believed he sent over a thousand résumés), had he not landed a single interview, let alone a job?

It was clear that where he was stuck was in the first hurdle. He couldn't get a call from a recruiter. Of the nine months he has been looking, only two companies had called him. This is where many job seekers think that the problem is his résumé because it is where he thinks is holding up the process. But he had a résumé writer revise his résumé twice before reaching out to me. He also ran his résumé through scans that claimed to put in the right keywords in this résumé to beat the application tracking systems. All this work yielded only two calls.

It wasn't that he was new to the job search process. He had fifteen years of experience under his belt, had hired many people for his own teams, and the last time he looked for a job was about five years ago, and he landed a job then. But to me, it was crystal clear where he was stuck and that was his dossier. Mark was frustrated and I heard a bit of desperation in his voice. "I need a new résumé, Cara," he said.

This is where many people get it all wrong.

Over ninety percent of job seekers who call me think they need a résumé. They think that a new résumé will fix their career search problems. However, that isn't what they need. Yes, eventually they need a solid résumé (and cover letter and online profile), but it isn't where they are stuck. They are stuck because they aren't clear on what their next step should be. They are trying to be all things to all people by filling their résumé with all their experience in hopes of someone reading through it and finding the nuggets of relevant experience. The problem is that recruiters cannot spend that amount of time on each résumé. When I first started recruiting, I would place an ad in the newspaper and in about a week, ten or so résumés were either mailed to me or dropped off at the office. I would read each one carefully to see which person might have the experience to do the open position. I connected the dots for the candidate. Today, with online postings and literally thousands of people sending in applications within hours, recruiters no longer have the time to connect the dots. Instead, if it isn't obvious that the candidate can do the job, the recruiter goes to the next résumé and asks the system to send a rejection email (I call this a ding letter).

Because we must connect the dots for the recruiter, the first thing as a career coach is to help your client take a few steps back and get very clear. This process starts with the very first call you have with them before they become a client—this is my initial strategy session—and where I get to know my future client. It is also when I decide whether this person is a good client match for me (more on that later when we are talking about the sales process). I take copious notes during my call with the prospective client. And the first thing I want to learn is the person's dream come true.

Notice that I said *dream come true*. I didn't say ideal job. The reason is because I want to learn more about the person's motivations, hopes, and dreams. Because the dossier I create for them must be with this entire picture in mind. If I didn't ask this question, I would never know that Derrick wanted to move to Boise.

Derrick was a brilliant I.T. guy. He was with one healthcare company for the past sixteen years and has climbed the corporate ladder. When I asked him what his dream come true was, he said, "I want to retire in eight years. See, I am forty-two now and I am going to retire when I turn fifty." That took our conversation in a completely different direction, and I asked a series of questions around his desire to retire at fifty.

I was curious—why fifty? Why not sixty? When I asked, he explained that he had a goal that by the time he was fifty-one years old, he would be done working for someone else. It was a goal that he and his wife had talked about for a long time. They would really begin to live after retirement.

"What are you going to do when you retire?" I asked. I had to know whether he was planning to open a business or if he wanted to fish all day! Was there anything he could do now that would set him up for that new adventure once he retired? He told me that his plan was to open his own outdoor recreational organization. He wanted to spend his days in the woods or the stream, testing outdoor gear or taking tourists on extended trips into the mountains.

"You live in Sacramento now, but at fifty where will you be?" I asked. I just assumed that he'd need to move, because one can burn through their reserves very quickly in California. Derrick and his wife had planned to move to Boise, where they could live comfortably near places where they can explore the great outdoors.

From these questions, it was clear that Derrick wants to move and live in a community where he and his wife could live off their well-stocked nest egg and just live off the land. With this end in mind, I could help him achieve his dreams. If I were just a résumé writer, and I did that for many years, I would just make his résumé look better. However, now that I knew his dream come true, my entire focus shifted to a life in Boise and what would he need to do now to reach his dream.

The strategy session is vital. It is where I begin to envision where this person is. How clear are they in their job search? It is when I see how many steps we need to take to help the person get really clear.

Once the person is clear and I am clear, I see a narrative of the person's path to that ideal role. It is the story that sings throughout the person's dossier so that when a recruiter lands on their dossier they say, "Oh, I get why Derrick is applying for our position."

I believe writing a résumé is mostly an art. Yes, there is a bit of science in the knowledge of solid writing skills. However, most of it is an art because the way the words lay on the page is just as important as the words itself. The design is half of the résumé because it is driven by the norms of an industry (manufacturing versus services) and location (New York City versus Boise).

A résumé that worked for Laura who lived in San Francisco didn't work for her in Colorado Springs. Laura is a Paralegal, and I helped her over five years ago. She emailed me recently in a panic because the résumé that got her two jobs in San Francisco was failing. I pulled up the last copy I had for her and understood why. The format that we used five years ago was directly geared towards jobs in Silicon Valley, not Colorado Springs which is a more conservative community. "Oh, that explains why the only company that called me was a start-up in Denver," said Laura. Sure enough, once we changed the format, Laura got several calls from recruiters.

However, what if your client doesn't even know if they are on the right career path? They wish they could be as specific as Laura was. They feel stuck because they aren't sure they know what they should do when they grow up, and they are already grown up. This process of helping someone identify their life's calling through their work is a dance. The steps are the same, but the tempo and style changes depending on where the music leads. Unlike the linear process of creating an eye-catching resume, helping someone identify their career direction takes a lot of questions and time for the person to reflect.

When I am helping someone identify what their career calling is in life, I divide up the time in three chunks. The first bucket I call "sitting on the rock." It is a time of individual thinking and self-reflection. A chance for a person to finally spend a bit of *me* time—time thinking about oneself—a luxury in today's world. During the period of sitting on the rock, my client does a bit of self-reflection. I addressed this process in my earlier book, *The Art of Finding the Job I Love*. To avoid repeating myself, I recommend you pick up that book so as to get the tools of what I mean by sitting on the rock. Once the client completes this self-reflection, then I start the dance, the discussion that leads to the work they were meant to do.

I first get them to talk about their current or last job. I ask, "What did you love about that job?" And capture at least three things that they really, really loved doing. I go into detail into each one, so I really understand the love. For example, this is my conversation with Lene.

"At Avis, tell me what you loved about your job," I ask.

Lene said, "I loved teaching people new things."

Not sure what Lene meant by that statement, I asked, "What do you mean teaching people? Describe this to me."

"I loved helping someone who feels like they can't hit their number hit it. I worked with one gal who thought she would never hit her daily insurance rate. I observed her and coached her, and quickly she was exceeding her goal. I love that," explained Lene.

I continued, "What else did you love?"

"I love achieving," said Lene.

Now I felt like we were on to something! "What do you mean, achieving? Do you mean sales?"

"Yes! I love to sell. I love hitting my numbers. I love when our office hits their numbers. I was always like that, I love it when there are goals," said Lene.

Bingo! I probed a bit more. "What if the company changed the goal, are you ok with that?"

"Yes! If I understand why, it is just another goal to hit. I am fine with changing goals," exclaimed Lene.

I didn't just take the first thing she said; I dug. And more than what I share here, I really dug deeper because I wanted to understand what was at the core of what she loved. Lene loves meeting goals, she loves the challenge of hitting a target. She loves the feeling of making a sale. I had a growing thought that Lene's calling in this world is in some form of sales. I then turned to what she didn't like.

"Tell me what you could do without if you could eliminate things from your current job?"

"I don't like the hours. We are retail and because we rent cars to people who travel to this city, we are open very early to very late and on the weekends. If I could work only Monday through Friday, that would be ideal for me. If I could have Thanksgiving with my family, I would be very happy. Plus, I love taking my dogs on hikes with me. I would love to have my weekends free, so I can spend it with my dogs out in nature."

I dug deep in the different things that Lene did not like about her job. She clearly does not like working weekends and holidays. That tells me that a retail job would not be ideal for her. She also loves being in the outdoors. That is obvious so that she can hike with her dogs. Soon jobs started to pop into my head.

"What about Customer Service Manager?" I asked.

Lene's lips puckered, and she said, "Yuck. That is the part of my job that I like the least, all of the complaints. I can manage fixing issues; however, to be surrounded by customer complaints all of the time I would not be happy."

"What about Inside Sales Manager?" I asked.

Lene pondered for a second and said, "Hmm, that is a possibility, but I am not sure I'd like to be in one building all of the time. But that could be an option."

"What about outside sales?" I asked.

"What do you mean outside sales? Like a roving sales rep?" asked Lene.

With excitement in my voice, I said, "Yes, like a Territory Sales Representative."

Lene's eyebrows raised a bit and she said, "Oh I think I'd love that. Do you know I have a certification as a pharmaceutical sales rep?"

"No, I didn't know that!" I exclaimed. This certification wasn't listed anywhere.

Lene explained, "It isn't on my résumé because after I got two certifications, I wasn't sure if pharmaceuticals were what I wanted to do. I've always been fascinated with how drugs affect the body. Since my college days, I love that entire aspect of drugs and pharmaceuticals, but still not sure if that is exactly what I want do so."

All the while we are talking, her dogs are barking the background. Something clicked, and I said, "What about an animal health territory sales rep?"

Silence. "Lene?"

"That is it. That is what I want to do."

We then pulled up three very different job descriptions that we found on the web of three different types of animal health territory sales reps. After reading all three, Lene was convinced that that is what she wanted to do next. Not only did she meet the minimum qualifications of the role, if we could design her dossier to point towards all her sales achievements, she could have a very compelling and powerful dossier.

Did you see the dance? You might think that you'd need a background in human resources or recruiting, but I reviewed this conversation with a director of children's camps, and she came to the same conclusion of territory sales rep without any prompting on my part. If you think you just do not have the background to help someone land on their career path, I recommend you join a career coach cohort community and use the collective voices in the community to help you help your client.

Once she landed on the role of sales, I asked her to find an ideal job description at an ideal job. That became my target job from which I created a compelling dossier that outlined all of her skills in sales and why she would be a rock star territory sales rep for the animal industry.

Now that your client has a beautiful and compelling dossier, the key is to somehow get your client in front of the hiring manager so that the recruiter will give them a call. Just applying online yields less than a ten percent return rate. If we can get two people to mention your client to the recruiter, the chances of getting a call from the recruiter goes up exponentially.

A few days ago, I spent a week with twenty-five executive recruiters. I asked them, "If you heard about a candidate from one person and they had the minimum qualifications, how many of you would call the person?" About half of the room raised their hands. I said, "Same person, same qualifications and now you heard about this person from another person, now how many of you would call that person?" All hands went up.

This is the power of a referral. Whether from someone the recruiter knows or not, if a recruiter hears of someone from two sources, the chances of your client being called is high. Your client may have a connection into the organization. And consider that you may also be a great person to nudge the recruiter for your client. You could reach out directly to the recruiter and pass along their résumé as a pro bono résumé.

I love reaching out to companies for my clients. It is my chance to really brag about them. George led three successful start-ups in Silicon Valley and made his millions. Now he wanted to have some fun without the intense pressure to raise capital, so he targeted chief product lead roles. There was one company that he was struggling to find inroads to networking, so I reached out to the founder and C.E.O. of the startup directly and sent an InMail through LinkedIn:

Hi Josh,

I'm not sure if you are searching for a head of product, but there is a guy who is really a gifted product person. He just rolled off of SmartUs as CEO and doesn't want to be CEO and instead wants to do what he loves and that is leading product. Here is his LinkedIn profile. Let me know if you would like me to connect you with him or feel free to reach out to him directly.

This was Josh's reply:

Hi Cara,

Thank you for reaching out to us at FreshNow and thinking of us. I would be very interested in an introduction to George. Would you be seeking a finder's fee?

He thought I was a recruiter. This makes sense, as I've led recruiting for years. I responded back that this is completely pro bono because I just love making recommendations of great talent these days. I connected George with Josh, and now he is in the third and final round of interviews with FreshNow. As a career coach, you can make these types of introductions to move the process towards your client.

Having a clear direction, a clear next step, is essential to having a compelling dossier. Often, I take clients back one or two steps and ensure the client gets very clear on what is their next step. Then with that in mind, I build a dossier that sings their narrative. Then we work on getting two nudges to the recruiter so that your client gets a call. Does this seem like a lot of work? It is. This is why applying online is easy but doesn't yield as much. It takes this type of focused work to increase the odds that a recruiter will call your client.

Next, we will talk about what your client should do to pass the next hurdle: getting an invitation to an onsite interview.

CHAPTER 6

How to Get Invited to an Onsite Interview

reating the dossier happens before anything else in the job search process. Your client could have such a solid network that they could get interviews without a solid dossier; however very soon in the process the recruiter will ask for a résumé. Up until this point, we are quite focused on creating their dossier, beginning to apply, and networking to get the attention of a recruiter. Once those balls are up in the air, we begin building skill to get over the next hurdle: getting an invitation to an onsite interview. This requires building skill in two areas. The first area is to create a system so that your client picks up the phone every time it rings and is prepared to speak with a recruiter 100 percent of the time. The second area is to begin preparing for interviews now. Not when an interview is scheduled, but now.

The number one most important task that your client must do when in a job search is to pick up the phone every single time it rings. It doesn't matter what they are doing or where they are; for the most part, it is imperative that the client pick up the phone.

Why?

We have a saying in recruiting: time kills all deals. The longer the process takes, the higher the likelihood that it will fall apart. We've seen this time and time again, and it is very frustrating for the recruiter. The hiring manager loses the budget. The candidate gets another job. The company goes on a hiring freeze. An internal candidate pops up at the eleventh hour. There are so many things that happen in an organization that if we don't fill positions quickly, there is a chance that it will not be filled at all. Because of this, recruiters move fast. At the point a recruiter is ready to screen candidates, the recruiter will have a stack of maybe ten candidates that look solid on paper. The recruiter will set aside a nice chunk of time to call candidates and will go through the stack of résumés. The recruiter expects to talk with about four in the stack if they are lucky. And in that first four, they'll like fifty percent of them, meaning about two candidates. The recruiter will then put together the candidates' documents and forward them to the hiring manager to review. That is round one, the first round of viable candidates, and now it is in the hands of the hiring manager to review both candidates and let the recruiter know which one to get to know.

Your client wants to be in round one. Candidates in round one have the most attention from the hiring manager. Most likely, the hiring manager will want to talk with both candidates in round one. It is at that point where the recruiter begins to divert their attention to keeping these two candidates hot—motivated to stay engaged in our recruiting process. Although still important, the recruiter isn't as focused on filling the pipeline with additional candidates, and it gets moved to the backburner. If your client didn't pick up the phone and missed being in round one, your client is now chasing the recruiter leaving messages and sending emails with a sluggish response. All the while, the other two candidates are moving through the selection process.

Ask a client if they've ever had a situation where they got a voicemail and they called the recruiter back only to never hear anything again. This happens often because they've missed their chance, and now the hiring manager likes someone from that first round and the recruiter is putting most of the time focused on the candidates in the first round. It is imperative, when you are in job search mode, to pick up the phone each time it rings. Driving? Pick up the phone and pull over to the side of the road. In a meeting, excuse yourself and take the call.

Now that your client is conditioned to pick up the phone each time it rings, the next important thing for your client is to sound like they are the only game in town. What do I mean by that? Imagine this exchange:

The phone rings.

"Hello?"

"Hi Lene, this is Jim, recruiter for Acme company. Do you have a few minutes?"

"Acme. Acme? Hmm, oh yes Acme!"

Jim is wondering, "What am I, chopped liver? She must be applying at a ton of other companies."

It doesn't start the conversation on a great foot. The reason why a client would pick up the call is because they can't possibly remember all the companies that they applied to. The companies' names are getting a jumbled in their mind and it isn't that they aren't interested, it is because they aren't organized. That is why I recommend that you coach your clients to have a very manual process to track companies.

Many clients use spreadsheets to track companies. That is fine; however, I recommend they print it every time they update it and put that printed document in a folder that they carry wherever they go. What else should be in that folder is a copy of their résumé and cover letter. And each time they apply for a position, to print out at least the job description. With these pieces of information (and practice mock interviews with you) your client should be prepared to have conversations when recruiters call. Then when a recruiter calls your client, they are on the ball and will make the recruiter sound like they are the only company they are interested in talking to.

Now let us talk about preparing for interviews. Why do I recommend your client begin this process as soon as possible? The most important reason is because if a recruiter likes what they hear over the phone, they may dive deep into the interview right then and there. The second most important reason is because the interview is the most important step in the process, and the sooner your client can begin preparing, the better their performance will be during an onsite interview. But, what questions should your client prepare for?

I asked a group of twenty-five executive recruiters and recruiters what their standard questions that they ask in a screening call are, this is what they said:

- Tell me about yourself
- Tell me a little about what you are doing now
- Why do you want to leave?
- Why do you want to work for us?
- What is your salary expectation?

These are the top five questions asked during a telephone screen. If the recruiter likes your client, they may dive right into the other questions normally prepared for a later conversation. Because we know with some certainty what will be asked, we should do our very best to help our clients answer these five questions.

My book, *The Art of Finding the Job You Love,* gives a methodology of how to prepare interview answers to the first four questions. It is a creative method to help your client integrate storytelling into their interview answers. Instead of rehashing what was mentioned there, as it filled an entire chapter, I ask that you look at that book for instruction. The last question requires a bit of research before formulating a response.

A recruiter will ask your client compensation one of two times. The first is early in the process. If compensation wasn't discussed then, it will be at the end of the process just before negotiating an offer. If a recruiter is asking at the start of the process, the recruiter is seeing if they can afford the candidate. They don't want to go all the way to the end of the process and then realize that the candidate is significantly above their salary range.

Many candidates think it is a negotiation tactic and will attempt to avoid answering the question. This is very annoying to a recruiter. I've talked with recruiters who will drop candidates that will not provide compensation information at the start of the process. They will think that the candidate is playing hardball and is being difficult. This is where it is important to ensure your client is ready to answer the compensation question.

This is my methodology to answering the compensation question "What is your salary expectation?"

1. Know what the market is paying. You can look at free resources like salary.com or payscale.com. You could also look at glassdoor.com or indeed.com; however, keep in mind that this information is self-reported. Get several datapoints to get a sense of what is market rate for the position.

2. If the person is under the market, research why. Did their organization not provide increases? Was it a start-up or small firm? Identify the reason for being behind the market. Your client should say something like this, "I am at $XXX and I am seeking to be at $XXX. I've been behind the market because my company is a small firm and did not provide annual increases. How does this fit within your salary range?"

3. If the person is above the market, research why. Is it a firm where it is in a really tough industry and has a hard time recruiting? Is it an unpopular industry? Or is it because the individual was always paid higher than the marketplace due to his/her expertise? No matter what, identify the reason. Your client could say something like this: "I am at $XXX and I know

I am well compensated. My firm is in an unpopular industry and thus needs to offer higher market salary to attract talent. However, I am very open. How does this fit in your salary range?"

4. If the person is competitive with the market, then the answer is fairly straightforward to the question, "What is your salary expectation." Your client should say, "I am at $XXX and know that it is competitive in the marketplace. However, I am open. How does this fit within your salary range?"

You can see a pattern. I am at $(insert amount). Statement of how it first in the market data. A statement that your client is open. And asking how it fits in the range.

The response from the recruiter will let your client know if they are in the range or not of the position. Be sure to say, "I am open," because that tells the recruiter that the client is flexible regarding salary.

Now that your client is prepared to answer these five common questions, I recommend they spend a bit of time creating a list of questions to ask the recruiter, if time permits.

When a recruiter or a hiring manager says, "I am setting aside twenty-minutes for quick chat," what that really means is that they want some sort of out in case the interview doesn't go well. They may have set aside more time; however, not wanting to set any expectation that the telephone call might go longer in case the interview is going in the wrong direction, it may be an easy out of a shorter call. But if the recruiter likes what they are hearing, the conversation may go well beyond the stated time and your client should be prepared to ask questions.

What questions should your client have prepared before the call? I recommend that your client have at least five to ten questions prepared for the call. The best way to generate this list is to ask your clients to put themselves in a space of being very curious. What do they want to know? Capture all the questions that flow and then from that list, pull out the top five to ten.

Some clients feel the need to conduct more preparation for telephone interviews. I agree that there might be times when preparation is a must, like for technical positions. If your client is targeting software development jobs, as an example, your client may be expected to talk about coding and languages. However, often clients spend too much time researching a firm before the call at the expense of preparing their answers. Most clients spend too much time researching company in preparation for an interview. This is often not the best use of time. Spend just enough time to find things about the company that are interesting and are in alignment with the client's passion or mission or purpose, write down a few important facts, and then spend the rest of the time preparing their answers to the top questions. However, this is one last statement I highly recommend every single client have ready. A mic drop statement.

A mic drop is the very last thing you say before you leave. It would occur after all the questions have been asked and answered and just before you end the call. To say something like, "I'd like to say one more thing. I am so excited just to have a chance to chat with you and dream a bit about being part of the organization. I have followed your company for many years now, and I know you have a lot of excellent candidates to choose from. I just want to say that I am so excited to even have a shot at it. Thank you so much." Mic drop. Work with your client to see what a natural and authentic mic drop would be so that they leave the interviewer with a very positive impression.

How can you tell they don't like you? If the recruiter says something non-committal like, "I have other candidates to talk to and so I'll get back to you in a few weeks with next steps." Then you know that you may not advance to the next stage. If the recruiter asks you if you are talking with other companies or is trying to schedule you to meet with the hiring manager, then you know that you're possibly moving to the next round.

Remember to send a thank you email the next day. Then begin to focus on other opportunities. Fill your pipeline because the ideal role might be right around the corner.

There are so many reasons why a company hasn't called back. The reasons are endless. It is easy to think that you blew it, or you said something negative. That isn't necessarily the case. There may be many reasons, internal reasons why they haven't called you back. The best thing is to help your client move on and fill their pipeline with other opportunities.

It seems like such a simple thing to explain to job seekers. The best way to move forward in the interview process is to pick up the phone when it rings. Recruiters aren't expecting the candidate to be ready for the call so if your client is a bit surprised, that is fine. Make the recruiter feel like they are the most important person to be talking to at that moment and settle in to be clear and concise. Leave the recruiting feeling like your client will make them look good if they presented this person to the hiring manager. The best way to do that is to be prepared with a small handful of answers to the top questions and prepare a quick mic drop answer. And when your client is invited to the onsite, this is where most of preparation is put to best use.

CHAPTER 7

How to Get an Offer

The onsite interview is where the rubber meets the road. This is where the offer decisions are made. And although it is only a small period of time, only one hour of your interviewer's time, it is showtime. It is the casting call stage where your client is putting on their very best authentic performance. I am going to share in this chapter tips and tools to help your client get a job offer.

In my book *The Art of Finding the Job You Love*, I provide tips on how to integrate improv in the interview preparation process. I recommend that you check out that book. In this section, I am going to review some of the other important pieces to help your client land the offer of their dreams.

So, once you've nailed the interview…what next? Sending a nice thank you email or sending a note card is a very nice touch. Although it is tempting to sell during this stage, I much prefer a simple thank you email filled with gratitude. I ask my clients to put themselves in a spot of gratitude and write a thank you email. Send it to me before sending it to the individuals. What I am seeing is the feeling or the energy that is coming through the email. Is it one of thanksgiving and gratitude or from a spot of scarcity and trying to still sell? I want to build this capability with the client so that they can feel confident in their future emails, whether we are connected at that time or not. Then, see if your client can add more activity to the top of their funnel. It may take a bit of coaching on your end to encourage them to fill their funnel, to take the time to do so when they are so close to receiving an offer. However, I've seen deals fall through too easily and that it is best to continue to fill the funnel until an offer is accepted and notice to resign given.

Is this an offer? "We are very excited in you as a candidate and would love to have you on board!" Until the company representative is discussing a starting salary and a start date, it may not be an offer. Because of this, I recommend that your client not give notice until a later date. An offer should come with specifics, like compensation, benefits, and discussions of a start date.

Below is a comprehensive list of items that may be negotiable. I recommend that you discuss with your client other benefits that may not be on the list and yet are important to them. The best time to use this list is when you are getting the verbal offer from an employer—as you are speaking with the employer—go down the list and ask the employer, "Could you tell me more about this…?" Or, "Do you have this…?" Your goal is to gather information. You are not negotiating at this point. Sound cheerful! Curious! Happy!

Start Date
- When would you like me to start?
  - Do not ask for a different day–you aren't negotiating anything at this point, and you want to come back with one (1) ask

Title
- What is the title of the position? Is it still the same?

Base Pay or Base Salary
- What is the base pay?
- Will I be an exempt employee or non-exempt?
  - Exempt employees do not earn overtime; while non-exempt employees do for any hours worked over forty in a week, and in some states, hours worked over eight in a day.

Bonus Pay

- Is there a bonus? If yes, is it paid quarterly, semi-annually, or annually?
- What are the criteria to receive the bonus?
  - ○ E.G., company meets revenue projections, or team objectives, or personal objectives?
- What is the targeted payout if I meet 100 percent of the objectives?
  - ○ E.G., it could be a percent of annual base pay, which is the most typical form.
- Of the people who are eligible for the bonus, approximately how many achieve 100 percent (this gives a sense of how hard or easy the objectives may be to get a payout)?

Commission Pay

- If your position is a type of sales role, you may have a commission.
- What is the criteria for the commission?
- When are commissions paid? Monthly, quarterly, annually?
- Of the people who are eligible for the commission, approximately how many achieve 100 percent?

Wardrobe Allowance

- If you are expected to target high-wealth clients, you could ask this question: is there a wardrobe allowance?

Other Incentive Pay
- Is there a Long-Term Incentive Payout (L.T.I.P.)? If yes, please tell me about the program.
- Stock options (the option to buy stock in the company at a lowered rate, no value until you exercise your option and buy stock), if yes, ask for information about the plan.
- Stock grant (given actual stock of the company, sometimes called R.S.U.s, restricted stock units, value once you receive the stocks), if yes, ask for information about the plan.
- Any other incentive pay programs?

Paid Time Off or Vacation
- How many hours or weeks do I earn in the first year of employment?
  - You care more about where you start as it should build from there. You could ask to see the P.T.O./vacation policy.
- Sick leave—*do not* ask about sick leave. It will feel odd to start out a new job thinking about taking off for work due to illness.
- Holidays—How many days of holiday are paid in a year?
- If you have already planned a vacation in the next twelve months, you could mention it now; however, better to mention it the first week you've started.

Major Benefit Plans

- What type of medical plans are offered? Could I see a price sheet to see what the premium cost is to employees?
  - ○ No two plans are alike. You don't have the power to change the medical plan, but you should know how much you may need to pay for insurance
- When am I eligible to start medical insurance?
- Do you have dental insurance? If yes, could I see information about the plans?
- Do you offer vision insurance? If yes, could I see information about the plans?
- What are other benefits that I should know about?

Tuition Reimbursement

- If this is important to you, ask if they offer this benefit, otherwise, skip.

Relocation Assistance

- Is there relocation assistance?
  - ○ If you are moving more than ~fifty miles for this position, you should ask the question.
- If there is, what is the amount?
- How is it managed? Is it expense reimbursement or lump-sum payment or through a relocation company?
  - ○ The most lucrative is a relocation company as the relocation company takes care of everything

and tacks on a margin and then charges the company

o The next would be a lump-sum amount that you can use for any type of relocation expense—it is basically a chunk of money—keep in mind that any lump-sum may be taxed at around thirty percent

o The most burdensome is when you pay out of pocket and submit receipts for reimbursements—per I.R.S. regulations—but, be thrilled that you have relocation assistance!

- Is there a housing subsidy?
- If you are not moving, but the company is expecting you to fly to the office periodically, you should ask these questions.
  - o If so, how much is the amount?
  - o How is this managed? Reimbursement? Or, company direct pay?

Sign-On Bonus

- Is there a sign-on bonus?

Retirement Plans

- Do you have a 401(k) or 403(b) plan? If so, when am I eligible to participate? Do you have a match program?
- Is there a pension program? If so, could you send to me information about the program?
- Any other retirement plans?

Life Insurance

- Do you have a life insurance plan? If so, can I buy above what is offered by the company?
- This is getting into the nitty gritty and I wouldn't recommend you ask unless you have a compelling reason to do so. Do you have a Temporary Disability Insurance plan? Sometimes it is called Short-term Disability plan.

Telecommuting or Flexible Hours

- Do you allow telecommuting?
- If so, does the company help set-up a home office?
- Is the telecommuting flexible or set days per week?
- Are there set office hours or is it flexible?

Dependent Care or Medical Care Reimbursement

- Do you offer a dependent care flex program?
  - o If you have small/young children, this may be important to you.
- Do you offer a medical care flex program?
  - o Allows you to set aside pre-tax dollars for different expenses.

Gym or Club Membership

- Do you offer a gym or club membership?
- Some companies offer gym/club memberships fully paid while others may offer discount memberships.

Staying Connected

- Is there a company mobile phone or reimbursement program?

- What type of device is it?

Transportation

- Does the company provide a car?
- Is there mileage reimbursement?
- Is there free parking near the location?
- Do you participate in a transportation flex program?
  - You can set aside pre-tax dollars to pay for select transportation costs, like parking costs, public transportation costs.
- Any other transportation benefits?

Severance Package

- Is there a guaranteed severance package if the company experiences a downturn or any situation out of my control?
  - (Any position at the C-suite level should discuss the option of a guaranteed severance package if something occurs that is out of your control–e.g., downturn, new CEO who brings in his/her people. Other roles that are highly compensated and in a risky industry should consider asking this as well.)
- If yes, could I see the language for this package?

This is a comprehensive list and I do not know of one company that offers all of these items. I recommend your client keep this list handy, and when an offer comes say, "Oh I am so excited, hang on one second so I can grab a pen and sheet of paper." Then your client can ask, "Do you offer XYZ?" And then ask, "Is there any other benefit or perk that I forgot to ask about?"

Long ago I made an offer to a Vice-President and she didn't ask about parking. It was an item that wasn't freely offered to all executives. I couldn't say, "Oh, you forgot to ask about parking," because I have a fiduciary responsibility to my company. So, she didn't get parking. Six months after her start, she realized that her counterparts had a parking card. By then it was too late to negotiate the item. Thus, I recommend that your client ask, "Is there anything else, any other benefit that I forgot to ask about?"

Once your client has the information, the details of the offer, your client should ask for time to consider the offer. Something like, "Thank you so much. Could I have twenty-four hours to consider the offer?" will work! If it's a Friday, ask for the weekend. If they agree, which ninety-nine percent of the time they will, your client should communicate the day and time that your client will call them back. And make sure your client sticks to it. Then your client should call you, their coach.

There are very few people clients can talk to about a job offer, an independent third party looking out for your client's best interest, is really, possibly, only you. Together with you, their coach, they should look at the information. Plot it on a spreadsheet or manually calculate how much money you will actually be earning. Are they needing to pay for extra things that they didn't in the past like a medical premium? Are they really moving into a better financial situation? Keep in mind there are things that are like cash to your client. Each person is different. Possibly working in a field that lights their heart, working from home, having zero commute, or an amazing future boss could be cash to your client. Factor these items into your calculations, then turn off your emotions and look at this analytically. The goal from this process is to come up with an ask.

For example, I worked with a client who was looking at an offer that was a higher base. But now he had to pay health insurance premiums. That reduced this new total from getting $30K more a year to $20K more. In order for him to be comfortable making this move, leaving his current job, was for it to be at least $30K more a year. He decided that he needed to have at least $10K more in the offer or he probably won't take it. We put together an ask for $15K and he communicated that ask once, in one neat package.

I highly recommend your client ask once. You could have multiple things on that list, but when you ask the company, ask once.

A long time ago, there was a guy that I made an offer to that went back and forth several times and this went on for two weeks. My boss got involved. His future boss got involved. His future boss' boss got involved. He did not start the relationship well and forever after that, we all wondered about him because of the way he negotiated. And every little thing was attributed to the age-old "We should've known." So that is why I recommend one ask.

Ask what you want and ask once. Now, it may take a few back-and-forth to finalize a deal, but you want to put it all on the table at once. When your client comes back with the ask, have data to support the request. For example, a different title and why. A different starting pay and why. Your client should talk with you and review these items so that your client feels comfortable with a justification.

What if your client is very happy with the offer as is? I recommend you have an ask. Ask for more money. Ask for more time off.

Why do I recommend this?

1. Whatever your client starts out with now will grow from that point. The higher the base, the more money over time earned.

2. They may be expecting your client to negotiate, and if your client doesn't, they've left money on the table.

Let me tell you about Gene. I accepted a job long ago without negotiating. They were thrilled. I was thrilled. Soon after I started, they hired a colleague of mine named Gene. He was struggling with learning technology and his job. In fact, he was kind of struggling with almost everything. Very nice guy. He didn't seem to be able manage stress very well. He was supposed to take departments off of my plate, but the leaders came back asking for support because it seemed like Gene couldn't handle the workload. I was teaching Gene about our H.R.I.S., human resources information system. He was furiously taking notes. Then it was his turn to show me that he could navigate through the system. And instead of entering an employee's I.D. number, he entered his own. We were now looking at his data and guess what? He was getting paid $20K more than me. A peer. I asked my boss about it. Of course, I did. I didn't go snooping. I explained the situation to her and do you know what her answer was? "Well, he negotiated. You didn't. We offered the same starting salary and you accepted. He negotiated."

In my twenty years of making offers, about seventy-five percent of the women I make offers to negotiate. Do you know how many men *do not* negotiate? In all these years, only one did not. ninety-nine-point-nine-nine percent negotiate.

Happy with the offer? Imagine that they are thinking your client would negotiate and offered at a lower level thinking that your client would come back. If they don't negotiate, they might be leaving money on the table that they were willing to offer.

Now let's talk about the ask.

When your client goes in for the ask, I recommend a telephone conversation vs. email. Avoid email at all costs, as you cannot control exactly how you will be received through email. Your client has a better chance controlling how they sound over the phone. Start out with tremendous gratitude.

"I am so excited. I can't wait to start. I am so lucky and grateful for the offer," Then simply ask. You're just asking the question. You're not demanding anything. Your evidence may be compelling; however, this is not a quid pro quo request. This is not a take-it-or-leave-it request. Simply ask like this, "I have a few items that I'm wondering about. None of these are deal-breakers. Is it possible to consider…?" Then share your items. Give your supporting evidence. And then close your lips. The tendency is for us to ramble. After your client has made the ask, listen, and take notes.

Now based on my experience, if there's a bit of wiggle room, they may say something to the effect of, "I'm not sure. I'll need to get back with you. I have to check with [insert a name], and I'll get back to you with what we might be able to do."

Now if the company can totally give what your client is asking, they'll say something to the effect, "I'm sure we can do something; let me talk with [insert name], and I'll get back to you." Then you know that you should have asked for more, but it is too late at that point.

If the company cannot do anything, they'll say something to the effect of, "I am so sorry. We've given you our best offer. Our style is to offer with the highest. Our highest amount is the best that we can offer," or something like that. Now if a company cannot go any higher, know that your client has done the very best to negotiate. It is what they can offer and if your client is ready to accept the offer, it is best to accept it at that point. Show your enthusiasm and gratitude with something to the effect, "Thank you so much for considering my request. I am disappointed that nothing can be done, however, I'm very excited to get started. Now that those items are out of the way, I can say that I accept the offer. Can I receive a written offer letter? Once I receive the written offer letter, I'll give notice to my current company and start the transition." Always get a written offer before giving notice.

However, if the company can go higher, if there's a wiggle room, or if they can meet your client's ask, end the meeting with something like, "Thank you so much. When can I expect to hear back from you? I'm so excited and thankful. I know that we can iron out these details and get started. I cannot wait." Now when the company calls your client back, ninety-nine-point nine percent of the time that is the highest they can go. Discuss with your client what his or her response will be with whatever they come back with. Consider the different scenarios with your client so he/she can accept at that time.

But, if your client isn't sure and needs to ask for another twenty-four hours, do so. However, in my experience sitting on the other side, I will begin to worry. I myself have begun to pull out other candidate résumés to be prepared if your client does not accept the offer. Your client is captain of their own ship. Just know that if they ask for another twenty-four hours, I will worry. And once that time period is up, your client must decide and give an answer.

I recommend that they accept the offer with something to the effect of, "Thank you again for considering my request. I am so excited to accept the offer. When can I expect to see a written offer letter? *Once I receive that offer, I'll give notice. Thank you so much and I'm so excited to get started."* The italicized portion of that language is to stress its importance. You want a written offer letter with the items that you negotiated. If the information is off, they may have written the offer before the negotiation. Bring the discrepancy to their attention, note that there are a few things on the offer letter that had just been negotiated, and ask for a new offer letter.

If there are a few items that are not on the offer letter, that the company does not typically put it on an offer letter, that happens because offer letters are often standard formats. They may not put that special thing that was negotiated. At that point in time, your client has a couple of options. I recommend one or the other, or both. Your client can follow it up in an email and confirmation or write the items on the offer letter in pen and initial the entry.

Oftentimes, clients feel that if they do negotiate, they will kill the deal. Clients feel that they will come across as too harsh or too demanding. However, by following these steps and simply asking, asking once supported with data, you're merely asking if it's possible. You're not demanding anything, you're just asking a question and with tremendous enthusiasm along the way. The worst thing they can say is,

"Sorry we cannot give that to you, but our original offer still stands." I once heard a candidate say, "This will be the only time we'll be across the table. Once we pass this point in this process, we sit on the same side." I really like that saying.

As a recap, the key is to gather information at the time of the verbal offer, and then decide what come back with by asking once. Help your client know what they will accept before the company comes back. Constantly show enthusiasm and remember, envision getting an offer early and often in the job search process.

When should I give notice to my current employer? I am asked this question quite a bit by my clients. My recommendation is to do that once the future employer gives the all clear to start. This might be after a background check is completed or your signature on the offer letter. My recommendation is to get clarification from the company by asking something like, "Am I cleared to start?" Once given the green light, give notice at the current employer.

I once coached a woman, Shirlene, who was trying to leave a large global telecommunications company. She was there for sixteen years and wanted to try her hand in a different industry. She received a verbal offer (not in writing) and immediately gave notice at her current employer. Unfortunately, the future employer had a difficult fourth quarter and went back to Shirlene to tell her that they would need to start her in Q2 of the coming year. This put her in a difficult situation as she had already given notice. This is why

I recommend you give notice only after you get an all clear from the future employer.

Long ago, I worked with a brilliant guy. He landed a job with Netflix and then became quite a handful to his current employer. He told the story this way: "I guess I started talking too much about Netflix that my manager pulled me aside and asked if I could leave earlier than my notice." There is a way to resign and my recommendation is once you have the all clear, to write a written resignation letter. The letter should be short and positive and say something like this.

> Dear [Manager's First Name]:
>
> I regret to inform you that I am resigning my employment. My last day will be XX/XX/XXXX. I have had an amazing time working here at XYZ. I've learned so much and am so proud of all that we have accomplished. Thank you very much for all of your support and leadership.
>
> Sincerely,
>
> [Your Name]

Have this document in hand and make an appointment to meet with your manager. Sit down and explain that you've accepted an offer at another firm and thank them for all of their support over the time. Tell your manager your last day and hand the written resignation.

It is preferred for you to meet with your manager in person. If there are unusual circumstances and that is not possible, talk with your manager over the telephone or on video call. It is the professional thing to do to have a direct conversation.

What if your client's current employer provides a counter offer? These are both tricky and simple at the same time. Almost all the time I recommend not accepting a counter offer. Your company knows that you aren't as loyal and that it came down to money to keep you. There may always be a hesitation in their minds regarding you and your loyalty to the organization. And most of the time, there is a reason why the person wanted to leave in the first place. It is often not about money, but some other cultural or managerial or directional question. These things don't change. The reason why you wanted to leave will still be there. That is why I, for the most part, do not recommend accepting a counter offer.

Now I've accepted the offer, now what? It is time to celebrate! We don't spend enough time celebrating really big things. Go out to dinner. Give yourself a gift, like a massage. A new briefcase. A new pair of links or shoes. Something to commemorate the transition. And then begin to think about how you can leave extremely well, and give yourself few days in between to transition into your new role.

CHAPTER 8

How to Set-Up Your Business

Warning. You're going to hate this section of the book. Most people do. It is about creating a niche for your business. A *niche*. There is so much research to support the fact that the narrower your niche, the more successful your business.

There's this gal who calls herself the "Widow Coach." She is a life coach who only coaches women who have lost their partners. Another gal is the Vet Recruiter. She only recruits for veterinarians and staff that support a veterinary clinic. Two hugely popular people in different segments. If they marketed themselves as a coach or a recruiter, they would definitely not be as successful. Your coaching business will become significantly more successful if you create a niche.

Does that mean that the widow coach with only work with women? Nope. She works with men, too. However, when she markets, she markets 100 percent to women. That is her niche.

Niches are attractive. What is yours? Here are a few that I believe would be phenomenal:

- Career coach for individuals with disabilities
- Career coach for women returning to the workforce
- Career coach for the LGBTQIA community
- Career coach for women
- Career coach for mid-career changers
- Career coach for new graduates
- Career coach for minorities
- Career coach for introverts

What is my niche? I know hundreds of people land on my website and say, "Heck, I don't care about loving my job, I just need a job." And they move on. That is fine. Because they aren't my niche. I work with people who believe they can love their job. That's my niche; helping you to find a job you love.

If I was just a career coach, I would not be as successful.

Creating a niche is exactly what we are asking our clients to do as well. By asking them to Identify Their Ideal Job, we are in essence forcing them to niche their job search process. There is tremendous resistance to doing this as you are feeling some resistance to do this as well.

We know that the more generic you look in the job search, the less attractive you are. The more specific you are in your job search, the more attractive you are. This is the power of creating a niche. What is your niche?

WHAT IS YOUR TRUE NORTH?

Once you have your niche, I recommend you write a statement that is what I call your True North. My book coach asked us to list our Canada and the reason why she selected Canada is from a directional perspective. Is the decision facing you and your business moving you north towards your goal or away? This is the big, hairy, audacious goal. It's your True North. I recommend you write a statement that is both motivating and challenging the same time. Here are a few True Norths from others that have completed The Career Coach Accelerator:

- Help 10,000 individuals in the military translate their skills to civilian jobs by 2020
- Touch 250,000 people by finding jobs they love by 2023

- Be on the *Today Show* talking about helping spouses of survivors–mostly women who lost partners who served in the military
- Support 5,000 job-seekers find better paying jobs within five years

What is *your* True North?

DIFFERENT FORMS OF A BUSINESS— WHAT IS THE BEST FORM FOR YOU

I'm so excited to talk about ideas on how to set up your coaching business. There are many ways in which you can set up your business. I'm going to tell you about what has worked for me. You, of course, can set up your business however you see fit, and I always recommend you speak with your C.P.A., local Small Business Administration office, or personal attorney. We will discuss these items in this module: structure of your business, naming your business, should you have a website?, what about a trademark?, logos, business cards, emails, payments, statements of work, and a small bit about dry legal stuff that is very important as you start your business. All of my recommendations follow the L.E.A.N. or M.P.V. start-up philosophy of the lowest cost outlay for the quickest start. You can start your business with the least amount of cash outlay. Yes, there are ways to do this with a ton of money. I'm going to share what I believe to be the least start-up costs delivering the highest amount of value to you and your clients.

STRUCTURE

There are several forms of business. I started as a Sole Proprietor where income and losses are added to your personal income. I stayed as a Sole Proprietor until I generated enough income to support an S-Corp. Many coaches form L.L.C.s. Each has a different structure, fee requirements, and protection for you and your personal assets. You should consider obtaining business insurance to provide additional protection. That's about all I am going to say on this subject because it is an important financial decision and one that you should discuss with your C.P.A.

Talk with your C.P.A. about what is a business expense, meaning what you can write off for your business. For example, I am here in Hawaii to give a presentation for business, so my entire trip is a legitimate business write off.

NAMING

When I started my coaching business, it was named Startingline Résumés. About three years after, I worked with a company in S.F. called Eat My Words to help me create a name. It cost about $1,000, and I worked with a very creative person from the company to identify options that could be my name. Before I selected my name, I worked with an individual to see if someone else owned the name.

He looked at the U.S. Patent Trademark Office (U.S.P.T.O.) website and conducted a search (which you can do for free). And he did a search of the URL.

Be careful which service you use to search for the URL. There are services that will buy the name you search and then turn around and charge you for the use. Do your research before using a service to search for unused names.

Once confirmed that the name was cleared through the U.S.P.T.O. search and URL search, I purchased the URL with an automatic renewal. There are many schools of thought around your URL, way too many to talk about in this module. All I can say is a.com is generally the best. It feels weightier and in the minds of most people, like a legitimate business. Any symbols, like dashes, are difficult for your clients.

All this is to say that it is a big, long, drawn out process, and one where you can easily spend too much time researching. That is why I recommend you do not spend time or money on your business name. If a name does not immediately come to mind, I recommend you use your first name and last name and tag on Career Coaching or Consulting at the end. It could be Cara Heilmann Career Consulting, or C.T.H. Career Consulting. My URL could be CaraHeilmann.com. Your name becomes your brand, and that is the strongest and most effective way to start—including being the most cost-effective.

When you use your name as your business, then you do not need to get a business checking account (which has additional fees and a higher minimum balance). You can have a Doing Business As name, or D.B.A. Talk with your bank or find a bank with zero fees with the lowest minimum balance.

Why do I recommend you not select a name now? The most important reason is that you are not your ideal client. A name that sounds great to you may not connect with your ideal client. Then one day in the future, when you have time and money, a name will land on you and you'll realize that it is what you should call your company. Then you can send an announcement to all of your former clients letting them know your new name (and ask for referrals).

WEBSITE

Now that you have your URL, I recommend you create a very, very simple website. The easiest system I've come across, and I've tried a few, is Wix. With all systems, there is a tradeoff. It is definitely limited once you are really deep into digital marketing, when your business is beyond the $100K a year mark, you may want a different platform. Up until then, it will serve you *very* well. You can create a free subscription and that will probably be all that you need to start. Now, this will not be a Wixhow-to module. If you decide to use wix.com, know that it is very easy to use as the user experience is smooth. And when unsure how to do something, use a search engine to ask your question, and you'll find your answer out there in the internet.

Very closely tied to your website is your LinkedIn profile. Much of the same concepts that you use to help your clients update their LinkedIn profile can be applied to your own. Some prospects will look at your profile in determining whether they want to work with you as their career coach. Is your profile clean, easy to read, and visually appealing?

TRADEMARK

Once your company website is up, and you have a company name that you want to protect, or a product that you want to protect, like the name The Career Coach Accelerator, I recommend you submit an application for a trademark at a national level—not state level—with the U.S. Patent and Trademark Office or U.S.P.T.O. In this, I recommend you use Rocketlawyer, LegalZoom, or some similar service to manage this process for you. For $300, an attorney will process all of the paperwork needed to submit and get your company name or product trademarked. It takes about nine months and having Legalzoom or something similar manage this process for you gives peace of mind.

Until the U.S.P.T.O. approves of the trademark, you can put a ™ next to the name you wish to protect. Once the U.S.P.T.O. approves the Trademark, you can change the symbol to the ®.

Let us talk about what you should never put on your website. Prices. Never. It is the number one way to lose clients. In fact, every single word on your website will lose you clients. Be as minimal as possible. Every word, every phrase is to be writing in the words of your ideal client. It should follow this pattern: one third of their problem in their own words, one third their dream come true in their own words (a little about you that could include a tip or two), and a one third a call to action. Every landing page, every email campaign, every marketing should be in this fashion. What is their problem in their words? What is their dream come true in their own words? A little about you or a little tip and your call to action (C.T.A.). Your C.T.A. is where people raise their hands showing enough interest to send you an email or complete a request—it is often an opportunity for the client to read an article you've written, for example.

LOGOS

You don't need one. This is another area where you could spend a tremendous amount of time and money. Unless a logo comes to you immediately, I recommend you use your company name and a unique font as your logo. As long as the font is timeless, your logo will be timelines. Then one day, an image will hit you or you will have time and money to work with a *real* design firm to create a logo for you. The reason why it is often a waste of your precious time and money is because you are not your ideal client. What you love may not be what your ideal client may be attracted to. And using your name with a unique font is truly all you need.

BUSINESS CARDS

I've found that business cards are becoming more and more obsolete. If I'm giving a speech, no one asks for my business card. If they want to connect with me, I tell them, "This is my phone number. Text me." Or, I ask, "What is your number? I'll text you my business information." Create a contact for just your business in your mobile phone and text your contact to them. I've spent serious dollars on business cards that are literally sitting unused. The only people that have asked for my business card have been other coaches and authors.

EMAIL

Let's talk about your email address. If you are going to use your name as your business, I recommend getting a vanity email, like, cara@caraheilmann (dot) com. This has worked for me for many, many years. It is truly timeless and professional. I do not recommend an email that ends with @gmail and avoid @hotmail, @aol, or @yahoo. It has been many years since I've created a vanity email, so I am sure it is much easier today. I recommend you do a search and see. It is going to be a small fee to have a vanity email. If you have a company name that is not your name, I recommend the @ be the company name. If your company name is really long,

I recommend you use a smart shortened version. If you have a URL, you can use your hosting service to create a company email address. If you own a domain, Google will help you create additional emails cara@ info@ service@ very easily.

PAYMENTS

Of fifty clients, one will want to pay with a check. I have them mail it to my business address or explain that many payment providers will connect with their checking account, like Stripe. There are *so many* different providers available today. Once in a while I have a client who asks to pay over the phone, which is ideal. In that instance, you may want to look for a service that will allow you to take payments over the phone through a virtual terminal.

STATEMENT OF WORK

A Statement of Work (S.O.W.) protects you. It outlines how you will meet the client's expectations and your expectations from your client. Many coaches *do not* have a S.O.W. as my program is more like an education program and with online courses, you wouldn't sign a S.O.W. Would you? I have a very brief outline of expectations that is sent with the receipt. What is more important is to discuss the expectations with the potential client prior to starting the engagement. This leads me to other legal matters.

Legal matters are completely out of my wheelhouse, so I recommend you obtain legal advice on your own.

RocketLawyer or something similar might be a perfect low-cost solution to many of your needs. For example, you'll want to have a Privacy Policy and Use Policy for your website, you can easily create through RocketLaywer or something similar. However, I do recommend you find a powerful business attorney, one that you could sign a retainer just in case you need a very heavy hitter. I have a very powerful woman-owned firm in Los Angeles that I signed a retainer with. It doesn't cost anything to sign a retainer; however, what that does is give you peace of mind that if something were to happen, you would have the biggest, baddest attorney on your side. And once you sign a retainer, they represent you. Most attorneys, before signing a retainer, will ensure there are no existing conflicts of interest with any of their other clients, because they cannot represent two entities if there is a conflict. This is why I signed with one early on; in case someone starts to try to push me around, legally, I know that this person could never be represented by my attorney of choice. That's my two cents about the legal stuff.

CONNECTING WITH CLIENTS

I use Zoom.com for all of my client calls because I want to see the person during the coaching conversation. This set-up requires focus and attention. No longer do I hear my clients distracted while talking with me. You can use any system, as there are many available. Freeconferencecall.com has video conferencing and I used this service for years before moving to Zoom—it is easy, and my clients say it is very easy for them, too, and that is key.

Many people ask about my video setup because the sound and video are clear. I recommend investing in a light, a webcam, and a microphone. There are many options out there from inexpensive to high-end professional gear. I am about to invest in another light, something that is softer and more diffused, having selected a ring light I'd be happy to tell you what equipment I use, just drop me a line or an InMail through LinkedIn. I keep changing the items as my business grows and the technology advances. Keep in mind that, depending on your computer and set-up, different equipment will work for you. How did I find my current equipment? I did an online search for "Inexpensive best equipment for YouTube video," to start and found many different options. Bottom line, the necessary equipment is a light, webcam, and microphone.

Be sure to keep in mind what is behind you. It really doesn't matter what it looks like as long as you are comfortable with it and what you are communicating with the set-up. I started using a green screen where I could change the background and, although I loved playing with the technology, I much prefer my real office. There are items that have become necessities, like a can of hairspray to keep me from fussing with my hair, and different lip glosses. You'll create a little stash of stuff like that too for quick touch ups.

For scheduling appointments, very early on I realized what a major waste of time it was for me to go back and forth in email finding a day and time. I started to use Calendly and after many years, still use this app. However, there are many options out there. I prefer Calendly because it is easy to use, is integrated with my Google calendar, and easy to integrate into landing pages. My recommendation is to not spend a lot of time selecting a scheduling app. Pick one and learn how to use it.

We covered a lot of ground in this section! It's all very important information so that you can see the fastest, easiest way to get off of the ground and start your coaching business. Give yourself a week to get all of these tools selected. Do not spend too much time researching the pros and cons because the most fruitful exercise for you to practice is the sales conversation. It is during the sales conversation when you see if you and the prospective client are a good fit. And don't worry, I am not going to teach you sleazy slimy sales techniques. Relax and sit back because my approach is very basic and is about love.

CHAPTER 9

How Do I Sell When I Hate Sales?

I'm so excited to share with you my philosophy about sales calls. I love doing sales calls! I didn't start out thinking that I would, and this has been the single area that I've grown in the most as an entrepreneur. Although I have a Master of Business Administration from Vanderbilt University and loved my marketing class, I never understood the finer tips of sales, thinking that it wasn't my area of expertise. Yet, every day of my twenty years,

I "sold" ideas and sometimes projects. But I never had a system or a methodology of selling.

In this chapter, I am going to share with you my philosophy of sales and a four-step process that has been very successful for me.

Step 1—Let them know they are in good hands

Step 2—Open up the conversation

Step 3—Communicate your value to the coaching relationship

Step 4—Empower their transformation

LET THEM KNOW THEY ARE IN GOOD HANDS

Imagine that you are going to see the doctor because your feet hurt. It is a familiar process of making an appointment, showing up for your appointment, filling out some forms, waiting to be led to the exam room, and waiting for your physician. You hear rustling outside the door and a knock. Your doctor walks in and after a brief period of pleasantries, the doctor begins.

This is a familiar process to you and because of that, you take comfort that you are in good hands. Imagine if your doctor walked in and spent the first 10 minutes chit chatting asking about your day, where you are from, where you live. You'd begin to wonder where this is going and probably begin to worry that you are wasting your time.

I recommend you start each strategy call with a very short period of pleasantries, "Is this the right time for our call?" and then get right into the conversation. Then I recommend you tell them how the conversation will flow. Working with a career coach might be a new experience for most and if that is the case, explaining how the conversation will run will give them a sense that you know what you are doing and are in charge.

This is what I say during the first minutes of the call:

I've read through your résumé and have some questions for you. Let me tell you how I run these calls. I want to get a better sense of you, your career thoughts, and learn what you have done to date, including what you think has worked and not worked. Let us spend the next 45-minutes in seeing if we are a good match to work together. I'll let you know what is going on over here with me. You can ask all the questions that you have. If we are a good match, great. If not, what recommendations do you have? How does that sound?

Over ninety-nine percent of the time, the person on the phone will be thankful that you are in control of the conversation. Once in a while, the person will not like that you are in control and immediately, I know that this person is not a good fit for me. How does it sound that they do not like that you are in control? It will sound like this.

> *Well, I just want to know how much it costs.*
>
> *No, that is not what I was thinking as I just want to tell you what I need.*
>
> *That sounds okay, but what I really want to tell you is this.*

If the person is not able to let me lead the conversation, I politely end the call because this person is going to be very difficult to coach. In the few times that I have worked with someone who balked at me being in charge with our first conversation, the coaching process was extremely difficult.

If the person is actually relieved that you are in charge, because they are hoping that you are an expert, then I continue the conversation.

OPEN UP THE CONVERSATION

This is where I want to understand two things: what is your dream come true and what is the strategy you are using to get your dream come true. The first space of understanding their dream come true takes about 15 minutes. I start by asking, tell me, what is your dream come true? Then I continue to probe until I have a firm understanding of their dream come true. What does this dream come true mean to you? How will your life be better with this dream come true? What will change for you with this dream come true? I give a recap once I have a solid idea of their dream come true and ask for confirmation.

Then I ask questions to understand the strategy they are using to get their dream come true. What have you tried up until this point? What do you think is working and not working? Is there anything you are getting for not landing a job?

All these questions are about identifying the gap between where they are and where they want to be. It is similar to the scenario of seeing a Podiatrist. Right now, I have this pain in my foot, it hurts really badly, I can't go to work, I can't sleep. If we solve that pain, I would be able to go to work, I would be able to sleep because there's nothing more uncomfortable than not being able to walk.

Now, if they have identified a problem that you truly believe you can solve, you want to get a handshake from them to make an offer. And for me, the handshake is always some version of the question, "Why bother?" You could be perfectly fine not solving this problem. Clearly, many people live their whole lives under employed. You don't need to get a job that you love. You could get a job that you don't really like? Why can't you just be happy here? And they will usually, at that point, come up with the real reason. And this is how it sounds. "To be totally honest, I don't feel like I'm contributing to my family and I'm failing my daughter because I'm not working. I feel like I am not a role model for her." I say, I have a program called "Find a Job I Love Program." When we get to the point when I am saying, "This is what I have going on here."

When I feel as if I understand their situation, that is when I say, "Okay, I get you. You want to do something meaningful that you love so that you can be a great role model for your daughter. I have a couple of ideas for you." This is now when you state your value.

COMMUNICATE YOUR VALUE TO THE COACHING RELATIONSHIP

The third part of the call requires this handshake, and the handshake is what's the actual problem you're solving for them in their words. Saying things in their words is a very powerful thing. When you begin to use their own words, you connect with where they are. I try very hard not to use my words, not to rephrase anything and instead use their words.

It isn't that they need to find a meaningful job. It is to be happy on Monday morning.

It isn't that they want to climb the corporate ladder. It is to feel like they are contributing to something.

It isn't that they want recognition of their efforts. It is that they want to feel good about what they do.

I say, "I think I get you. You want [their dream come true in their own words], and I have a few ideas for you."

The third part is talking about ideas; the solution to their problem. It is not six weeks of coaching. It is all benefits to them. Say something like, "I can help you get unstuck. I can help you get clear. I can help you create documents that highlight your skills. To create a profile so recruiters find you. To connect you with executive recruiters in my network. To get you prepared so you are feeling really prepared. And so, when you interview you put your very best foot forward and they see all of you and can't wait to have you on board. How does that sound?"

I want to get a confirmation from them that I am actually solving their problem and that we're on the same page before I make any offer. Then, I will tell them the results: "At the end of the eight weeks, you're going to be clear on your next step, you're going to have a finished résumé, cover letter, and LinkedIn profile that tells your story. You are going to have a networking plan and be prepared to answer interview questions. You are going to know what you need to do to land a job of your dreams."

You need to know at least three to four results for them. What are the results they're going to have? Not how you are going to get them there. Focus on their results. And then, I might ask a question like, "How do you think having these things and knowing what you need to do to get a job you love will help you?" I want to make sure we're totally on the same page before I'm making any sort of offer. And until I get the next handshake, I am not going to give them any logistics.

I've just told them the results. At this point in the process they may have questions on how we will get these results. I ask something like, "What questions do you have for me?" This is the point when I listen and answer all of their questions. "What questions on how we get this done?" Close my lips. If they have no questions, do not put questions in their mouth. If they don't have any questions, it is a nice way for them to say that they aren't interested.

If they actually wanted the result, they would ask a question, probably this one: "Okay, so, how does it work?" And ninety-nine percent of the time, that's the question I get. "How does it work? What's the next step? When does it start? How do I pay you? How much is it? How long is it? How do we work together?" These are all signs that they want to buy

Generally, the three reasons people don't buy are:

- They don't really want the result…someone may be urging them to get a new job but in reality, they don't want to want the result, even though they may be telling themselves that they do.
- They don't believe that you can get them the result.
- They don't believe that they can trust themselves to do the work. They don't believe that they can get the result. They aren't worthy of it. Or it is easier to just

stay where I am now and not put in the extra work or face rejection in a job search.

If they ask those questions, "How much is it?" "What is it?" "When does it start?" "How does it work?" At that point, they trust you, they trust that this outcome is possible, they actually want it.

Then say the cost. Get used to saying that price and don't say a price that you're not comfortable with. My business coach says when asked, "How much should I charge?" She says, "The amount you can say without throwing up and not a dollar more." When I first started out, I wanted to charge $3,000 but felt really uncomfortable with that amount. So, I'd say, "$3,000, but I am offering a discount of $1,000. I also have a payment plan where we break up the amount in half and it is $1,000 each payment."

I offer some sort of timing parameter. For me, because it is just me, I can only take on a certain number of job seekers at once. I'm usually full of one or two people rolling off the program at a time. I say, "I have one spot now. Would you like to take that one spot?" If they ask for more time, I tell them that I have other calls and that chances are the spot will be taken very quickly. This timing parameter is called "scarcity" in sales. Having some sort of nudge that gets them to make a decision. It could be a discount that will end or a class that only has one more spot.

Bottom line for me is it is all about love. Do I feel connected with this person? Can I see myself helping this person? Are we a good match?

What if they aren't a good match? How can you gracefully exit a conversation? I chatted with someone who wanted to be invited to my accelerator program. We have a minimum requirement of ten years of work experience with a higher education degree or a life experience that would be a perfect niche, like an individual with a disability helping others find jobs. This person I was chatting with didn't have the ten years nor the degree nor the life experience. What I did was say that I didn't think he was a great fit for our program, and that I had a recommendation of another program that might be a better fit. One that was much more fundamental. I passed along that program's information to this person and he thanked me very much and said he would give them a call.

If I feel like I can help them, and we are a good match, then I empower their transformation by asking for payment.

EMPOWER THEIR TRANSFORMATION

I ask for payment over the phone or payment within a very short period of time. I do this because I know they are stuck and want to get unstuck as soon as possible, and I know I have the space to support them now. I do not know if I will have that space next week. The longer someone delays taking this crucial step of handing over their credit card, the easier it is to talk themselves out of taking that step. Because I want them to move forward in their job search, to get their career path unstuck, I ask for payment right over the telephone.

You may have noticed that my four-step sales process is the L.O.V.E. process and it is exactly that. This is how I got over my own weird feelings about selling. I see each sales conversation as an opportunity to see if we are a fit to work together and if we are, to empower that person's transformation so that they can start to feel good again about their career and their direction. To give them hope that tomorrow will be a better day and that you'll be there at their side coaching them along the way.

CHAPTER 10

When Things Get Hard

There is a book for entrepreneurs called *Guts and Borrowed Money: Straight Talk for Starting and Growing Your Small Business*. This chapter is all about the guts. Starting a business can be a scary thing. When faced with mounting bills and the new shingle you've hung as a career coach, it is easy to just get a job. I've done this twice. I left my corporate role at a nationwide healthcare organization and about six months into starting my career coaching business, a woman called me. She offered me a Chief Talent Officer role. It was right in front of me. And so, I put my shingle in a closet and accepted the job. Within a few months I was miserable. Then my friend offered me a V.P. of Operations position for a human resources consulting firm and I accepted the offer. It was much easier than starting a business. And within a few months realized that I missed my clients so much that nothing felt fine. I finally quit that job and never looked back. What's been key to me is to get a strong handle of my amygdala.

Do you know your amygdala? The amygdala is an almond-shaped part of our brain's limbic system adjoining the temporal lobe of the brain that is involved in emotions of fear and aggression. It is the fight or flight part of our brain.

When we were five years old, it may have saved our lives. Instead of running across a busy street, your amygdala said, "Whoa, whoa, whoa! Mommy said to hold an adult's hand."

It works for us even today as adults. When you get that creepy feeling where the hair raises at the back of your neck if you walk into a situation and something just feels off—that's your amygdala.

Our amygdala can be very helpful. However, the trouble is it cannot tell which situations may be life-threatening or just exciting new ventures. The threat is real to your amygdala whether you are walking in the middle of a dark street and you think a guy is following you to thinking of a new career. All it knows is that there is risk, that you are embarking on something risky.

Its job is to keep you safe. But often (especially if you live in a safe part of the world) it can keep you small.

There other names for the amygdala. I've heard people call it Negative Nelly, the little devil on your shoulder, or your saboteur. I'd love to hear what you call the amygdala. For us and our clients, the threat of something may cause our amygdala to go into high gear.

This module is to talk about different tools that you can use to help both you and your clients recognize the amygdala and quiet it down.

The first thing that has helped many of my clients is to name it, like I did earlier by asking you what you call your amygdala. Depending on your client's background, you can accomplish the same thing by calling it the negative voice in your head or incongruence with your vibration, as Abraham Hicks calls it. There's a wide range of spiritual beliefs and I've found it helpful to understand where my client is coming from. I do ask, "What is your spiritual background?" when talking about the amygdala so I know what would sound more like their language. For example, I had a client who said, "I grew up very Catholic; I call it the Negative Nelly."

I personally like to stick to the scientific terms, like amygdala. It's the anatomical name. It is more comfortable to me. You can manage this however you want, what is comfortable to you. In fact, it might be speaking to your client niche—mine is executives, so saying something like "incongruence with your vibration" might not make sense to them. But if your niche is reiki healers, for example, saying "incongruence with your vibration" might make total sense.

First thing is when I am sensing someone's amygdala is getting in their way. It sounds like I shoulda, I couldha, and I woulda. It's a negative spin. For some people it *is* a spin. They can latch on to what their amygdala is saying and go and on.

It really starts to come out when they are trying to articulate their ideal job. "I'm really scared of…" and "I'd love to do that, but…"

That's when I say, "This is a perfect time to talk about the amygdala."

I've found that the more attuned I am to my own amygdala, the easier it is for me to hear other's.

The key is to learn how to quiet your amygdala. I believe the amygdala, when left unchecked, can lead someone down a path of despair, depression, and worse. And the job search process can be very depressing.

In many ways, I am a life coach entering someone's life through the slice of career. I'm helping them with something vitally important to them in a time that can be quite depressing. So, it is important for us to help them with quieting the amygdala, so they can land a job of their dreams.

When we can quiet this part of our brain, we experience a profound sense of peace, joy, and happiness.

There are so many resources out there to help people quiet this part of their mind.

- Eckart Tolle, The Power of Now
- Don Jose Ruiz, The Four Agreements
- Esther Hicks, author and speaker of workshops on the law of attraction
- Brooke Castillo, Self-Coaching 101
- Thanks for the Feedback by Stone and Heen

And many other favorites. So, here's what I do to help my clients tame their amygdala:

1. Recognize its voice
2. Learn to shut it off
3. Do 1. and 2. faster and faster

I could tell something was really bothering James. His eyes had a far-away distant look. "Anything you want to clear before we start?" I asked. Clearing is a term used in coaching to give the other person an opportunity to say what is on his mind so that he can focus on our conversation. James looked at me like he was seeing me for the first time and told me about a mistake that he made a work that day.

"I missed it and now my team needs to put in extra hours to mix the error," James lamented. "The worst thing about it is that my boss's boss is now involved. But at least it is being fixed before it is sent to the client."

We continued with our coaching meeting and finished on a positive note. Two weeks later, during a call with James, he gave a heavy sigh.

"What's up?" I asked.

James said, "Oh, I'm thinking about that error again."

He'd been carrying around that error, that burden, for two weeks. The world has moved on, yet James was still there at the realization of his error. I actually said, "James, are you still there?"

The first step to ending the spin is to recognize the amygdala's voice. I do this in various ways:

1. I point it out when I am hearing it.
2. I challenge my clients to focus one day on trying to recognize when it is speaking, keep a journal, and write down what it is saying.
3. I ask if there are physical manifestations to the amygdala like clenching jaw, tapping finger, etc.
4. We draw a baseline chart.
5. I ask the client, what are you feeling now? Any negative feelings?

The second step is to learn to shut it off.

1. The sheer fact of recognizing the voice is sometimes enough distance for people to shut it off and say, oh, there I go again.

2. Analyzing the type of thought, as if this is an evaluation type of feedback, as described in *Thanks for the Feedback* by Stone and Heen.

3. Take a deep breath.

4. Meditate.

5. Pray.

6. Sing or worship.

7. Exercise.

8. Keep a journal.

9. All of these things help us to stay present!

The third step is to learn to do this faster and faster. Brooke Castillo wrote a book called *Self-Coaching 101* and introduced a methodology called C.T.F.A.R. I find it to be a very quick way to quiet the amygdala. It teaches us how to change our feelings by changing our thoughts in a way that is lasting.

- C stands for Circumstance
- T for Thought
- F for Feeling
- A for Action
- R for Results

1. Write these letters on a piece of paper exactly as above, down the left side of the page. What is the

circumstance. This is 100 percent fact—zero feelings or thoughts about the circumstance.

2. Under that, I write my thought about that circumstance. This is my thought filled with emotion and my perspective on the circumstance.

3. Then below, what are my feelings about my thought of that circumstance.

4. Below are my actions based on my feelings.

5. And below that are the results based on my actions.

6. Immediately next to this, or in a different colored pen, I write another thought, a completely true thought but one that makes me feel better. This is the toughest part of this exercise.

7. Once I have a new thought, a true thought that makes me feel better, I list my feelings.

8. Then my new actions.

9. And then the new results.

This process has helped me in the moment end the negative self-talk. The first time I tried to do this, it took me about ten minutes to complete. Now I complete it in seconds.

I do not think we ever completely eliminate the amygdala from doing its job at warning us, because it can literally save our lives, but I do believe we learn how to shorten the time it takes to recognize the spin and quiet that part of our brain.

So that we live in more moments of peace, happiness, and joy.

New coaches ask how long it takes to get the business up and running. For me, it lingered for a bit until I hired a business coach and started working with someone who understood my business and had a successful business of her own. My business coach's fees were $50K, and she helped me turn my business into a $300K business. It was a very worthwhile investment in my book! Once I started under her coaching, my business took off, and within three months, I was in the black and in six months, I was turning a very hefty profit and hiring my first employee.

I have new coaches ask me when they should leave their current jobs to become a career coach. I've put together business plans to help them make the transition and, the more determined they are to make the plan work, the faster they're able to transition to a full-time career coaching role. The key is to put together a plan and to execute that plan. To keep your amygdala in check and keep your eyes on your True North, the reason why you want to become a career coach. I see my job is to bring happiness back into work, one person at a time.

CHAPTER 11

What's It Like on the Other Side

Long ago, when someone said that they'd continue to work even if they won the lottery, I used to think they were lying to me and themselves. There is no way one could be that in love with their career that, even if they won the lottery, they'd continue. I can honestly say that is the case for me. Every single day is a Friday for me. I love what I do. I love the people I support. I love hearing they got jobs, that they understand how this all works, that they are happy in their new roles. These things are all like money to me. It's like a million bucks just fell into my pocket.

One of my clients, Charlie, created a memory board of her True North. On her board are images of her ideal clients, people that she's helped that have loved each moment helping them. Words like "Love my job" and "Happy to go to work" are in her memory board. You can create a memory board. Put it in front of you to remind you each and every day the reason that you are a career coach.

Another client named Natalie has a connections box. It is a frame where she can put names of people that she wants to connect with, as well as images of people and business cards. Natalie uses this box to put out her intentions. Create a connections box with things and people that represent your ideal client.

I live by my calendar. I do whatever it tells me to do. Because of this, I make meetings with myself. If I know I need to work on business development, I make a meeting with myself with a label of sales. Then when the time comes, I go straight into doing that item. This process is what my mentor, Glen Furuya, owner and CEO of Leadership Works, said is flag on path. Put flags on your path; for me it is my calendar so that I do what is important for me and my business.

One important item on my calendar is time for my walks and runs. Make your health a priority. I know that if I don't put this in my calendar, I won't do these things, and the business of the day will just sweep me away. So, I schedule time for me to do self-care. Working out, eating well, resting between heavy coaching sessions, getting my nails done, getting my hair done...all these are important self-care things so that I feel good about the way I look and look as good as I feel.

Remember that you are meant to do this. Not everyone is called to be a coach. Not everyone is called to have fun side by side with someone, helping them in their careers. If you've been called, honor that voice and lead. You were meant to do this. To be part of people's lives and in some cases, the darkest of their days, to support them in dreams to get a job that they love. To put food on the table and love the job they do to earn that money. Remember that you are called and meant to be a career coach.

Acknowledgments

Someone once said, if you want something done, give it to the busiest person you know. Writing this book was proof that this is true. From the publishing of my first solo book to this one, I saw Ready Reset Go® explode. We moved all our learning modules to a learning management platform to help scale. We launched The Career Coach Accelerator® to train more people to become career coaches. Our staff grew from me to a team of 8 and rejoiced when we hired our director of business development. Jumping from intensely fulfilling coaching calls to meeting with my marketing team, I couldn't shake the feeling that there are more people out there in exactly my situation where it feels almost by accident that they were meant be a career coach. Between calls and a few stolen days here and there, I wrote this book. And it was written with one person in mind, Michelle. She was the inspiration for this book and in fact, this book is one long love letter to her with a purpose of giving her tools and hope that she can do the same and have a thriving career coaching business. Thank you, Michelle, for being there with me on each and every page.

To Angela Lauria who not only helped me get my first book published but became my business coach. I am not sure where I'd be without her help. Thank you, Angela, for having the right things to say at the right times to keep me marching towards my Canada.

Special thanks to Moriah Howell, my editor for always making me feel like every word I've written has value. To Cheyenne Giesecke, thanks for being even busier than I am and still making the process seamless and easy. Many more thanks to Rae Guyn, Ora North, and my house captain Amari Ice, for being part of the journey.

To the Morgan James Publishing team: Special thanks to David Hancock, CEO & Founder for believing in me and my message. To my Author Relations Manager, Margo Toulouse, thanks for making the process seamless and easy. Many more thanks to everyone else, but especially Jim Howard, Bethany Marshall, and Nickcole Watkins.

To my best friend and husband, Edgar, I thank you for being my one constant. I look at the picture of us on my shelf of the night you proposed to me at Liza's in Natchez Mississippi. I've pitched a million different businesses since then, and yet when I said, I'm going to be a career coach, a smile lit your face and you knew, as well and I that I finally landed. Thank you for being my IT guy, my finance guy, my everything guy.

And to my two boys, Eric and Andrew I'm glad for the little moments that you let me into your very busy high school lives: windshield time in the car, reviewing your English homework (my contribution to your education), and watching NFL Red Zone together on the couch. I smile when I hear you tell your friends, "My mom wrote a book" and hope that it inspires you to bravely step out and do what you want to do.

About the Author

Cara has helped over 700 people get jobs they love. Prior to launching her career coaching business, Cara was VP and executive of talent acquisition teams for large national and international companies—ARAMARK, Kaiser Permanente®, Baxter Healthcare—and small- to mid-sized firms from Silicon Valley start-ups to staffing agencies. Now she brings happiness back into the work world by helping people get jobs and trains the next generation of career coaches.

Cara is Founder and CEO of Ready Reset Go®, a career coaching firm helping people find jobs they love and training coaches to do the same. Ready Reset Go® helps job seekers get clear on their next career step and have that narrative sing through the documents to the interview, so that companies see all that they can contribute and can't wait to bring them onboard.

Cara is a best-selling author of *The Art of Finding the Job You Love*, and co-author with Brian Tracy, renowned author of the best-selling book *Ready, Set, Go!* Cara consults at companies to build internal career coaching teams that both manage recruiting and reductions to retain talent by redeploying them within their own organization.

Cara has a Master of Business Administration degree from Vanderbilt University and a Bachelor of Business from the University of Hawaii. She is a certified Senior Professional Human Resources, a Certified Professional Résumé Writer, a Certified Professional Career Coach, and on the FORBES® Coaches Council. She is also Lominger Recruiting Architect® and TRACOM® Group Social Styles certified. She is on the Board of Directors of Wardrobe for Opportunity, a nonprofit in Oakland ending poverty by helping individuals get a job, keep a job, and build a career.

Cara resides in the San Francisco Bay Area with her husband and two boys where she runs throughout the east bay hills training for marathons and crazy fun 24-hour relay races.

Cara loves to hear from people, feel free to connect:

www.linkedin.com/in/caraheilmann/

www.readyresetgo.com

@CaraHeilmann

Printed in the USA
CPSIA information can be obtained
at www.ICGtesting.com
JSHW082354140824
68134JS00020B/2068

9 781642 795912